MOUNTAIN DAYS
AND
BOTHY NIGHTS

Dave Brown and Ian Mitchell

MOUNTAIN DAYS
&
BOTHY NIGHTS

By

Dave Brown and Ian Mitchell

Luath Press, Ltd.,
Forest Bank, Barr,
Ayrshire, KA26 9TN.

First Edition: 1987
Reprinted 1988
Reprinted 1989
Reprinted 1992
Reprinted 1993

Typeset and designed by Luath Press Ltd.
Printed and Bound by Dynevor Printing Co. Llandybie,
Dyfed.

CONTENTS

What to put into it?   Page 1

The Caves of Arrochar   Page 11

Lochnagar and the Royal Bothy   Page 23

A Weekend Across Country   Page 39

Bothies Fabled   Page 57

Glencoe   Page 71

Dreadful Dosses   Page 99

Skye   Page 113

Beinn A Bhuird and the Secret Howff   Page 125

Ben Nevis   Page 139

Bob Scott's   Page 151

A Winter's Day   Page 165

A Winter's Night   Page 175

This book is dedicated to those pictured within.

WHAT TO PUT INTO IT?

The party had climbed the hill, despite the bad day, and then descended to the bothy. The bothy was far from being palatial accommodation. So bad, indeed, was it that people were said to have preferred the sheep fank opposite. The bothy log book, however, explicitly forbade use of that alternative, and insisted that the dismal doss be used. The floor was liable to flood when snow drifted against the outside back wall and then melted. This the new inmates learned as they watched sodden shirts and a loaf floating away over the cobbled floor, as if trying to escape out the door. It can only ever have been a day bothy, and never a permanent dwelling. A small fire burned in the hearth. Since there was little to burn in the vicinity, heather roots and sheep shit provided a smelly reek for the company.

As is only too often the case in Scottish hills, the weather was rotten. Early winter snow was melting; the ground was a quagmire and the path into the bothy had been turned into a raging burn. Cold grey sleet was now falling. A party of four sat on a battered settee (imported from God knows where) that gave out a musty smell. Since it could only really seat two, two sat on the arms, and the comfortable places (also nearest the fire) were taken in rotation by the party. This game of musical seats helped keep circulation going.

The older half of the party, who generally tried to prolong their occupancy of the cosy recesses of the settee, were on the wine of the country. Amber nectar in copious quantities was finding its way down their throats. They were flanked by a pair of 'halflins', who occasionally and disrespectfully demanded their turn on the more comfortable parts of the settee, and who were imbibing quantities of orange juice. Charitably, their partners interpreted this as manifesting a desire to retain their faculties to absorb the wisdom that would be dispensed as the evening wore on.

1

But it was difficult to keep the conversation going; as difficult as it was to maintain the fire. Sitting with damp feet in a cobbled puddle, one of the mature duo broke the silence, and tried to flog the conversation to life. 'This is miserable, but for a' that, the misery does mean something. There's tales to be told, craft to be passed on, lessons to be drawn. The next generation, like these shavers here, needs a bit o' depth. Otherwise it'll all become clinical and technical, a go-faster, Goretex world.'

Ears were pricked up at this, and the youths momentarily forgot their claim to comfort, as the initial sally brought forth a reply.

'A book, that's the thing......A bothy book,' said his companion, now happily sailing on a whisky effluvia. 'Mountain punditry, and tales oft told round bothy fires — but real fires, nae like this ane. Tales that will open doors, but nae bothy doors. Hotel doors, feather beds and hot baths. The life o' a gentleman climber on the royalties.'

His companion in menopausal fantasy jumped up, waving an arm. 'Aye, an' trips tae Lunnan, tae discuss wi' perfumed decollette wummin publishers a' about the dialectics o' the mountain class struggle. They love that doon there: they like a bit o' rough.'

Each fantastic bid seemed to invite a rival out-bid. His companion came back with, 'And in oor auld age, fan we just stroll the glens, pittin' oor noses roun' bothy doors and chatting indulgently wi' the youths, we'll meet young blades telling tales fae oor book, and pass on wi' a gentle smile.....'

This was interrupted by a riposte from one of the orange juice brigade. 'And there'll be a wee plaque one day, on the door there, announcing that *The Great Bothy Book* was conceived within these walls.'

'That's typical o' youngsters nooadays. No respect. No ideas themsels, no crack, a' they can do is mock. I mean, orange juice! Where's the tradition there? They'll be daein' press-ups on the flair next. The least youse could dae is tae mask some tea for your elders and betters, while they discuss serious business.'

The Doorway

The youths went good-naturedly, one for water, and one to the table to light the primus. As well as ensuring some sustenance, this manoever removed the competition for the cosy seats, and allowed their occupants to stretch out a little, and lean on arms hitherto occupied by half a dowp. A musing silence descended, and then the flights of fancy began again.

'We could dae it though. There's hunners o' books about mountaineering in Scotland, but naething about bothies and bothy life. And we've got...' He calculated quickly, 'mair than 50 years o' experience between us. We could dae it.'

From the vicinity of the now roaring stove came the half-mocking 'Whit'll ye pit intae it?'

'Jist you get on wi' the tea, and leave the weighty matters tae the grown-ups. And bring a lump o' cake while ye're at it. A man could die o' hunger here.' The novice continued with his efforts, which imparted a cheer to the gloom, a cheer that was augmented when his companion returned with a fence post, which immmediately went on the fire. 'I found it in the sheep fank,' he announced, proudly.

'Aye, its wunnerfu' whit they teach them in the Tenderfoots nooadays,' was the sole praise which issued *de profundis* from the settee.

'Right enough, though, fit will we pit intilt? People want epics. They want finger-jamming gyrations and sagas of the loose tricouni. We canna gie them that. I mean, we've done a bit, but nae *that*.'

The fence post crackled as it burned, and the flame lit up the face of his companion. Its lines deepened in the fireglow as he thought, then replied, 'Naw, there's hunners o' books like that. A lot o' ego tripping that the mass o' mountaineers cannae share. I think they just look at the pictures and ignore the text. Some o' yon writing is afae bland. Nobody has written for the great middle ground. Those who've done a bit o' bothying and some climbing and walking, and done it for years, or those that's setting out tae dae it. We've got tae say whit the ithers havnae said, tae manufacture a tradition for the

4

broad masses o' mountaineers, excluding the day trippers at wan end and the tigers at the other.'

'Bothies in particular, naebody's written aboot them, and fit gangs on in them. And Scotland is unique in the number o' open dosses and howffs, that gie an alternative tae club huts and youth hostels. I bet maist bothy users dinnae even ken how they got there. We could pit that intilt.'

'Well, how did they?' came the inquiry from the tableside, from the tenderfooted log-finder. A stunned silence of mock outrage greeted this. What, was there a man here under false pretences, so philistine as to give no thought to the origins of the shelter he was using? But the bait had been taken; they now had an audience.

'Jist you bring that tea here, young man, and yer auld dad will tell ye aboot bothies.'

The company was arranged again on the settee, of whose recesses the older duo now had unchallenged possession. After pausing to ensure attention, one began. 'Ye probably think they've aye been here, or that they biggit them because they kent ye were coming? But bothying is a fairly recent development. The early climbers and mountaineers at the turn o' the century were from a select social group. They got their accommodation in hotels, or the lodges o' the lairds.....

'Mind you,' objected his partner, 'sometimes no. Robertson slept at Ben Alder cottage, and Seton Gordon used Corrour Bothy, though baith were inhabited then.'

'Aye, aye, wheesht and let me get on. Even in the 1930's, fan the number o' mountaineers expanded dramatically, there was still little bothying. Read Borthwick's *Always a little Further*, and ye'll see that camping and hostels was fit they used then.....'

'That's no' right. Dan Mackay's barn in Glencoe was an open bothy in the 30's — Borthwick used it. And people like Nimlin and Humble were howfing in the 30's.'

Let a man get a word in edgewyes. Ye've heard o' the Highland

Clearances? Or did ye nae get that in the Tenderfoots? Well, these glens were originally full o' people, clansmen. But as the chiefs turned tae sheep and deer, they cleared the glens. But they had tae build cottages for the new shepherds and gamies, and Lodges for themselves for hunting. This lasted till about World War Two, and then the second Highland Clearances took place, and it's this that led tae bothying. Aifter the war, ye had Land Rovers and bulldozed tracks for them. The lairds didnae need their workers oot in the wilds ony mair. They could ship them in and oot, cut doon on wages and cottage maintenance.'

'But there was also the Hydro and the Forestry, paying big wages. Folk wernae willing tae work for the lairds' wages after the war.'

'Look, fa's telling this story, you or me? So these cottages were gradually abandoned. Ben Alder in 1940 or thereabouts. Luibeg (though that's nae a bothy), as recently as 10 years ago. The habit o' dossing in the buildings that were abandoned started naturally, withoot any organisation. But then ye had vandalism, bothies disappearing up their ain lums, and the wind, rain and snaw takkin their toll.'

'And then the Mountain Bothies folk came in and started organising everything, wi' their daft wee lists o' bothies, encouraging folk tae flood intae bothies that were hardly used years back.'

'I cannae agree wi' ye there,' came the response of his grizzled comrade. 'Its wrang tae think that informal groups could maintain bothies, there has to be organised maintenance. The bothies that we use —that you use — would hae gone by now, but for the M.B.A. It's true that there's a lot mair folk gyan tae the hills, but they'd be gyan onywye. Affluence and transport means the hills are busier. Its true ye meet folk now that act as if they ain the bothy, and winna pass the time o' day wi' ye. Folk that never say "Come in aboot the fire and hae a cup o' tea." But its nae M.B.A. maintenance that leads tae that.'

The argument seemed to carry some weight, for his partner

replied: 'Aye, maybe so. But still, they're class-collaborationists, working wi' the lairds.'

'You use words like bothy, doss, howff — what's the difference?' asked one of the youths.

'A bothy's an auld hoose, like a cottage, that's become empty and is maintained as climbing accomodation. It comes from the old word for a farm-labourers dwelling. A howff is a much simpler structure: a cave, a few rough boulders or a simple, purpose-built shelter, like Slugan Howff.'

'Slugan Howff? What's that?'

'Oh, ye'll have to read the book to find out!' was the reply. 'And doss is just a word used to cover anywhere you sleep, be it bothy or howff.'

'You could put that about stand-offish folk in your book', opined one of the youths.

'We'll put that in oor book a' richt, and a lot mair forbye,' was the reply.

By now the fire's attempts to continue burning were increasingly feeble, and the party retired to their sacks, occupied with their own thoughts. In the morning the sky was lowering with sleet, and a wind blew coldly. The party decamped, and began to trudge back to waiting cars. As the younger half sped towards the col, the others, still a little under the influence of the malted barley, followed behind.

'Ye ken, it's a guid idea. There's lots o' thing we could pit intilt.'

'We'll need a few epics and routes, though; folk expect that. And try tae work in the Queen, sex and dogs, that aye sells books.'

The col was reached as sleet began to fall, and the descent towards the glen floor was made, with a torrent underfoot.

'One thing we'll pit intae it is that there's mair tae it than trudging up and doon daft wet hills,' came, between puffs, another contribution.

'There is mair, or there was. There was the appprenticeship. Ye learned things by daeing them, by going away wi' folk that kent, and introduced ye tae bothies and mountain craft, by practical example.

And ye built up the tools o' the trade as ye went along, making do with, and even making gear, and buying the real stuff piecemeal. Nooadays, they come ontae the hills anonymously, after passing through Outward Bound Schools and the like. They're a danger tae life and limb. They cannae decide whit tae dae in a white-oot till they look up their Langmuir. They're gaitered and Goretexed from heid tae tae the first time they go on a hill, even if its Bennachie or the Campsies. They go aboot in wans and twos. If its raining, they gang haim. They're very functional aboot it a', and there's nae guid crack in them.'

'The big groups have gone, for sure. Another thing that's gone is the identity o' being a weekender, every week in life nearly, and no jist a day-outer. There was the group loyalty and cameraderie that built up. Ye knew that ye'd meet yer pals at certain pubs or bothies. And the transport was collective. Ye took the buses, and ye'd have a guid crack at the back, wi' a bevy on the wye oot, and stopping for chips on the wye haim. Then somebody would get a van, and away ye'd go, in the days before the M.O.T., nae brakes and baldy tyres, a dozen or so o' ye singing in the back, no feeling the cauld.....'

'That's a bit romanticised, surely.'

'Maybe for you dour East Coasters, but no' for us men o' the west. Your personalities were warped by the Cairngorm Hills, hunners of miles fae the road, wi' nae tops. You never went past the Devil's Elbow, and if ye did, naebody would understand that funny language ye' speak, wi' yer "Foos and fits, and loons and quines".'

This was too much of an assault on honour to be ignored.

'You West Coasters are great at getting intae the boozers, but nae sae guid at getting oot and ontae the hill. The hills ye frequent are only staggering distance frae the pubs, and a' yer bothies are visible frae the road. Jacksonville, now, that's yer idea o' heaven, but till you've been tae Bob Scott's or the like, ye're nae a real mountaineer. Ye even ging camping tae avoid a walk! Camping!'

As they plodded on downhill through a Forestry Commission

plantation, insults were exchanged in the same vein. The cars finally hove into sight, a mile or so beyond the forest stile, where a rest was called for.

'Why did ye no' drive the damned thing up tae the gate?'

'Maybe its us that's changed. As ye get aulder, ye get mair cautious and plan better. Disaster, the stuff o' adventure, comes less frequently. Numbers whittle away and social interaction gets muted. Ye re-define your objectives, pleasures become quieter than those o' frenzied youth. They've got tae, or ye'd gie up.'

'We could pit that intae it. And the constancy that the hills gie ye, however your life changes. Even the worst weekend gie's ye something tae remember, some pleasure.'

Over the stile they went, and on to where the other two waited. Minds were working on ideas, silently now. As they reached the vehicles, one of their companions asked 'How's the book going?'

'Mock a' ye like, but ye wait, we'll dae it.'

'What's going into it?'

There was a pause as a pair of packs was deposited on the ground. Then: ' "Whit's gaein' intae it?" ye say. The things that arnae in ither books!'

Here is what was put into it.

The Narnain Boulders

THE CAVES OF ARROCHAR

Strung out untidily around the east side of the head of Loch Long, its shoreline often covered with tidal debris, Arrochar has only two obvious claims to fame. These are extravagantly superior toilets, and a magnificent view of the deservedly popular hill called Ben Arthur, better known as the Cobbler — 'The Jewel in the Crown of the Arrochar Alps' — as one wit from the Glasgow climbing fraternity used to call it.

The Cobbler occupies a unique place in the history of Scottish climbing, for it was the focal point of its 'great proletarian revolution'. This was the time during the '30s and '40s when the young Clydeside apprentices and their unemployed counterparts took up the then largely middle-class sport of rock climbing, in order to escape the dreariness of the dole or the mundane world of work. It was on the Cobbler, in the late '40s, that the great genius of John Cunningham and his Creag Dhu contemporaries first became apparent, and it was there that Hamish MacInnes, probably to the dismay of many traditionalists, started experimenting with pitons and other pieces of ironmongery that look suspiciously like bits of motor bike.

Today, with most climbers and walkers having access to cars, the Cobbler is a place to visit only for a day. However, in the 1930s and up until the 1960s, many people, eager for time on the hill, relied on boat, bus or hitch-hiking. As those methods of transport were slow and required relatively high expenditure of time, the Cobbler, when you got there, was a place considered worthy of a weekend's attention. For many such week-end adventurers, accommodation was a problem. True, the Scottish Youth Hostel Association had a hostel in Glen Loin before they moved down the Loch to Ardgarten.

But hostels cost money, and then there were all those rules and regulations. Tents could have solved the problem, but tents were a luxury that even the employed could not afford, and anyway they were heavy and they had to be carried about.

With hostels and tents excluded on the grounds of cost and inconvenience, attention turned to shelter that was both handy and free. Some favoured the loft of a barn belonging to a generous local farmer called Mr. Paterson, and though it was popular up until the mid-1960s, it was considered to be a rather unheathy place to stay. Crossing the courtyard could be hazardous. A young climber, tired from a day's work or hiking, could be attacked by small hairy dogs intent on savaging his heels. If he survived that, he then climbed the dark stairs to the evil-smelling loft where, more likely than not, he could be confronted by some of the biggest and boldest rats known to man. Unabashed by the new arrival, they would continue about their business — stealing loaves of bread from hikers' packs, racing around the corrugaged iron sheets that covered the holes in the rotten floor, or holding wrestling contests that used to keep everyone awake at night.

Regulars at the loft used to talk about those rats as if they were merely another group with whom they shared the accommodation. Indeed, it used to be said that they wore 'Bunnets and boots' — attire that was common to all the habituees. Others did not see the rats in the same light. One group, thinking about spending a night in the loft, turned back down the stairs when they saw the beasts. On walking away, one of their number held out his hands in the exaggerated manner used by disappointed, if not entirely honest, anglers when describing the 'one that got away', and was heard to say, 'Imagine being feart of wee things like that!'

The other aspect that used to put people off the barn was that if the loft was full, there was always the temptation to sleep in a hay wagon that stood directly under the landing at the top of the stairs. The danger was that the young athletes, faculties impaired because of over-refreshment in the local bars, used to crawl out of the loft onto the landing to be sick on the innocents below.   Even the rats were not too keen on that behaviour.

The barn declined in popularity, and was dealt a lethal blow one fine summer's morning when one of its regulars appeared at the bottom of the crags on the Cobbler's North Peak with large red lumps on his body and face.   Among the horrified onlookers was one man who, despite the fact that his medical expertise was based only on a recent reading of a book about the Black Death, nevertheless felt confident enough to declare that the poor guy must have that disease, and that he must have caught it from the rats in the loft.   As the afflicted one ran down the hill in terror to find a doctor, the others in the stunned crowd vowed never to use the barn again.

For those who wished to avoid such accommodation made sordid by rats and delinquent climbers, the solution lay in the many caves and stone shelters found in the Cobbler area.   Most of these involve an uphill climb, but for those who did not want to expend such energy, or if the weather was bad, the obvious choice was the collection of caves and boulders known as the 'Arrochar Caves'.   These are found by following the Sugach Road, which starts near the police station on the north side of Loch Long, round to the forestry workers' wooden houses.   From there a dirt road heads up Glen Loin, turning left then right before passing a white cottage which used to be occupied by a forestry worker, but which now looks like somebody's holiday home.   The end of the road is marked by a gate beyond which there is a pylon.   From this a path leads diagonally through the forest to the caves.

The journey to the Caves after nightfall was, at one time, made very hazardous by the existence of a very old and obnoxious forestry horse, whose idea of a good time was to gallop at unwary travellers as they crossed his field.   This only happened at night, and many a hiker was frightened out of his wits as he heard the thundering hooves approaching from an indeterminate direction through the blackness of a moonless night.

On one such night a small band of climbers were making their way across this particular field with the aid of a torch so useless that it gave about as much light as a red-hot nail, when suddenly the surrounding silence was destroyed by the approach of this demented nag. The panic and confusion of the torch-holder was not helped when one of his companions asked for the torch. Thinking that his friend was going to save them by doing something fabulous and brave, like flashing the torch in the eyes of the malevolent creature, he handed it over gladly. The trust of this optimistic fellow was not rewarded, for as soon as his friend had the torch, he disappeared into the darkness, leaving the others to scatter in blind panic, hopefully out of the way of the approaching disaster.

The Caves, a wonderfully strange and convoluted place, though full of dampness, were extremely popular in wet weather. They not only offered shelter and wood for comforting fires, they also provided the bored climber with a variety of difficult 'boulder problems' on which he could practice his craft. The chambers most often used for sleeping in are found at the top end of the Caves, and to reach one of the most popular simply turn left at the end of the path described above. Where progress is blocked by a large rock wall, the cave is on the right. By passing through this chamber and into a rock corridor, one comes to the most famous of the Arrochar Caves. It is instantly recognisable as the large rectangular gallery in the rock about halfway up the left hand face. To gain access to it some simple rock climbing must be done up the arrete on the right. Inside, the floor of the cave is split into two, and on the upper level of the left hand side near the back, there is a small hole which, with a bit of a squeeze, allows access to an underground chamber. From here an easy descent can be made to a small underground loch. Back in the rock corridor, it is possible to follow this around to another popular chamber used by generations of climbers as a bedroom. And, indeed, although the recent growth of forest makes it difficult to follow Borthwick's description, this may be the cave whose social life in the 1930's was so vividly recreated in his book *Always a little Further.*

There are some disadvantages in using the Caves. Water has to be carried over very rough ground from the stream to the north-east of the main chambers. Sometimes the caves are very damp, and they can drip during wet weather, with the result that the accommodation, even the large caves described above, could be a lot less spacious than would at first be thought. Moreover, in order to avoid the drips, would-be sleepers often found they had to lie in a very contorted fashion. Despite these drawbacks, weekends in the Caves were always lively, for there was always plenty of people with whom to share a fire, sing songs and swap tales of derring do. The breed of men who spent their time there were not the kind who were only interested in the climbing, and who would therefore disappear back to Glasgow if the weather was inclement. On the contrary, they considered themselves not mere climbers, but 'weekenders' — men who enjoyed getting out into the country and living rough. They took pride in their ability to make themselves comfortable in adverse conditions, and they enjoyed the company of like minds with whom they could have a bit of 'crack'. Because of this, initiates hungry for tales of mountain characters and adventures could, in those caves, first hear about Tam's crowd and the great bus conductress pie assault caper. Or they may have listened in awe to the almost mythical tales of the trials of strength between Wee Davy of the Creag Dhu and Big Jim of the S.M.C. Another favorite they might have heard was the one about Black Rab and the Burning of the Boat.

If they wanted to escape the dampness of the Caves, a small party could always make their way up the path on the right hand side of the Allt Sugach burn. At about 300 feet above the floor of Glen Loin, diagonally across from a large rhododendron bush, they would find a delightfully dry cave that accommodates three or four people. This cave used to be called the Secret Doss. Hikers and climbers new to the delights of the area got to hear about it from more knowledgeable kindred spirits who, on assessing the genuinesss of the newcomer, would tell him of the secret, warning him 'It's a Secret Doss, so keep it under your hat.' After some time, however, the newcomer would find that this was not exactly the best kept secret in the world, for almost everyone he met knew about it. The location of the cave is

15

even described in the latest rock climbing guide to Arrochar, so the Secret Doss is no secret any more.

Not everyone wanted to stay down in the glen, and the weather was not always so bad that shelter had to be sought in the Caves. For many, fine weather meant shouldering a full pack and heading up the hill to stay under one of the boulders found in what was known as the Cobbler Corrie. One of the most popular of those dosses is found under the most southerly of the two huge Narnain Stones, which, during some primeval disruption, must have trundled down from Ben Narnain to their present position on the east side of the Buttermilk Burn on the present-day path to the Cobbler.

Unfortunately, no-one seems to use this as a doss nowadays. The protecting wall which used to leave only a small hole for entry has been broken down and the floor, littered with debris left by thoughtless day visitors, is very muddy. Up until the mid-1960s, however, this place provided a solid and dry shelter for the mountain traveller and as a consequence it buzzed with life after other visitors had dropped down into the glen below.

The principal pastime of an evening was contests of strength and balance upon the hard problems found on the boulders. Here the dictum that climbing is a non-competitive sport was proven to be false. Groups of climbers tended to concentrate on one problem at a time, each member having a go in turn, watched intently by the others. Not only did the climber have to contend with the difficulty of the problem, but his concentration was usually assaulted by 'advice' which was designed for the amusement of the onlookers and the distraction of the combatant. Thus, just as he would be inching his left foot towards a minute hold, eyes full of sweat, arms rapidly disintegrating into painful and useless appendages, he would hear someone enquire about the stability of the foot on which he was standing. Often this was enough to send the unfortunate climber clattering down onto what could be a muddy landing.

The sleeping accommodation under the boulder was limited and had to be carefully arranged, with the smallest being slotted into the tapering recess at the back of the cave. Such a claustrophobic position was distasteful to some, and there is a famous story of the time when five young Glasgow climbers packed themselves under the stone for the night. Everything was peaceful enough until the small hours when everyone was wrenched from sleep by a cry from deep within the recess. *'The boulder's falling! The boulder's falling!'* With hearts thumping in their chests each man suddenly threw his hands against the roof in an attempt to stop the imaginary catastrophe. Then, realising that they must have looked very peculiar lying on their backs straining to stop, with their bare hands, a multi-ton piece of rock from falling on them, they simultaneously burst into laughter that was both hysterical and relieved.

A few hundred yards above the Narnain Boulders the path to the Cobbler crosses the Buttermilk Burn, and then climbs the hill above diagonally until it attains some flat ground. Above is a rather rotten, shallow gully that splits a rockface in two. About halfway up the gully, on the right hand face, is a slight overhang which gives some protection to a sleeping platform known as 'Martin's Doss.' Martin, the man who made this place his own, was a burly, wild-looking chap who hiked around the Arrochar hills dressed in a Glengarry and kilt. He must have been hardy, for this doss does not give much protection from the elements. Accordingly, 'Martin's' was not all that popular, used only when other dosses were occupied, or by people who had run out of steam when heading for the 'High Doss'.

However, it was occupied one moonless night by a bizarre group of climbers who professed a belief in black magic. They were always going off into bothies with their black candles and their inverted crosses, saying the Lord's Prayer backwards in order to get old Beelzebub to show himself. Maybe they wanted to sell their souls in exchange for being good climbers, but whatever it was they were never successful in their enterprise.

On the night in question, the Narnain Boulders were occupied by some lads who were a bit sceptical, not only about black magic but also about the converts' strength of belief. To test their theory, they waited until it was quite dark before making their way silently to the flat ground below Martin's. There they spread themselves out in a semi-circle. Each man had a torch and periodically he would hold it under his face and turn it on for a few seconds. On the platform above the occupants were too busy with their hocus-pocus to notice at first, but unease began to creep through the group as one by one they caught a fleeting glimpse of a light-distorted visage apparently suspended in dark space. Eventually, after several sightings the mood of the group changed from unease to terror, and finally one tall, skinny lad with a pimply face began to croak: 'Lads! He's here — that's him!' This apparent but unexpected success of their devilish practices threw them into a terrible confusion, and as their hidden tormentors slipped away in the dark, there followed a heated conversation about what they should do.

The next day the outcome of their debate, along with an account of the night's happenings were reported to their apparently naive 'friends' from the Narnain Boulders. Much to the latters' suppressed delight, they heard how it was decided a sacrifice had to be made, and that a particular wee, harmless man should go out and confront this apparition. He went out reluctantly, protesting all the time, his eyes like silver dollars. And of course he found nothing. Despite this, the events of the previous night were reported with some satisfaction by the Martin's crowd, who saw it as some kind of vindication of their beliefs. The others merely nodded and kept the secret of the apparitions to themselves.

For those with the serious intent of climbing on the famous crags of the Cobbler, the High Doss seems to be an obvious choice of accommodation. The High Doss is the collective name for the two high altitude residences found under the two largest boulders of the corrie formed by the Cobbler's Centre and North Peaks. These are probably the best caves on the hill, not only because of the standard of protection from the elements afforded by them, but also because of the access they give to the many fine climbs on the Cobbler. The South Peak boasts Nimlin's Direct, Bow Crack, Ardgarten Arete and

Gladiator's Groove, while among the very finest of the North Peak are the Recess Route, Chimney Arete, Echo Crack, Direct Direct, Wether Wall and Club Crack. The last named is a very hard climb famous for the fact that, until recently, it had only been climbed by members of the Creag Dhu Mountaineering Club. Worth a special mention is Punster's Crack with its awkward step across the void at the crux, and its spectacular yet not difficult final wall. This is the one to impress the tourists on the summit of the North Peak. Through the clatter of camera shutters the climber may hear one of the admiring audience breathing the accolade, 'Wow! A human fly!'

The first belay on Punster's is a big block of rock. Above it is a huge overhang, split by a crack that widens as it goes higher. It used to be known as the 'wooden overhang' because an early attempt at climbing it was made by trying to insert bits of wood into it. This development in artificial climbing was made by two men who hauled a log of wood up to the first belay of Punster's. The leader then climbed up to the crack carrying with him a measuring tape. With this he would measure the width of the crack at an appropriate point, shout the measurement down to the second, who, using the block as a work bench, would saw the desired section from the log. The second would then pass the freshly sawn piece of timber up to the leader, who would hammer it into the crack and attach a sling to it. By standing on the sling he was able to move up and make another measurement. Although this attempt failed, it is interesting to note that this development occurred long before it became accepted practice in the mountaineering world to use pre-prepared wooden wedges as artificial aids.

The attraction of the High Doss was that by staying there parties could complete a number of climbs before those from the lower regions had even appeared.   And, in the evening, instead of bouldering at Narnain, or boozing in the Arrochar bars, they could finish a climb and watch the sunset before descending to tea, biscuits and bed, replete with that special combination of tiredness and contentment experienced only by the very fortunate.

It must be admitted, however, that not all the people who used the High Doss were gentle mountain philosophers. Some of them had a pretty hard outlook on life. At one time when money for climbing gear was tight, it was felt by some that the gear of climbers killed in accidents was 'up for grabs'. According to one story from the early 1950s, some lads were climbing a route on the North Peak called Right Angled Groove, when the leader slipped and crashed down onto the steep grassy ledge at the start of the climb. The noise of his involuntary descent attracted the attention of the lads at the High Doss, who started to run up the hill towards the unfortunate wretch, one shouting 'I'll have his bits', another 'Bags me his jaicket', and so on. These rather cruel shouts must have penetrated the shocked state of the fallen leader, for, despite the pain of two broken legs, he got up and while staggering about began to shout, 'I'm no deid! I'm no deid!'

It seems to be the case that the High Doss is not used much nowadays, and this is a pity, for it provides a unique mountain experience. Here many young climbers first learned what it is to live close to the mountain and observe its changes of mood. Early morning sunshine and late evening afterglow could be enjoyed in that solid silence that exists in the space between the last and the first of the day visitors. Even bad weather can be sensational up there, and some can tell of nights of spectacular electric storms when the thunder seemed to come from the very innards of the mountain, and the lightning created day from the darkness.

The experience of this mountain life stood in good stead those who, in later years, travelled further afield to the Alps, the Rockies and to the Himalayas. On one trip to the Rosengarten area in the Dolomites one such group of Glasgow climbers, working on a very tight budget, scorned the luxuries of the Italian Alpine Club huts, cheap though they were, in favour of a cave near a main path. The Italians had seen nothing like it, so they crowded round talking to the cave dwellers and taking photographs. Some, obviously thinking that people forced to live in caves must be poor souls, left money in the lads' enamel tea mugs. Their fame spread and friendships were forged with local guides and climbers. Invitations to huts for big plates of spaghetti and litres of wine followed. Then the guitars would come out. Skiffle was very popular then and one of the Glasgow boys played a mean Lonnie Donnegan. The Italians loved it, but then that is a whole bunch of stories for other times.

The Gelder Hut

LOCHNAGAR AND THE ROYAL BOTHY

Lochnagar is one of Scotland's most famous mountains, due to its association with Royalty since the time of Queen Victoria, and to Byron's famous couplet:

Oh, for the crags that are wild and majestic,
The steep frowning corries of Dark Lochnagar.

It is probably also the mountain most loved by North-east mountaineeers, who would echo the words, less exalted than Byron's, of one of the great Tom Patey's songs:

Masherbrum, Gasherbrum, Distegal Sar,
They're very good training for Dark Lochnagar.

For the adventurous, Lochnagar offers unparalleled scope for rock-climbing. Despite the the pioneering efforts of Raeburn and others round the turn of the century, Lochnagar was later rather neglected. This was in spite of the assertion by J.M. Bell, after he had ascended it in 1941, that 'for difficulty, narrowness and steepness', Eagle Ridge was 'altogether superior to any of the well-known Ben Nevis ridges.' It took the post-war generation, led by Patey (who burst to fame after conquering a cornice on the much-attempted Douglas-Gibson Gulley in 1950, and made the first winter ascent), to really demonstrate its potential. Since then it has offered many a young tiger the chance to earn glory.

Lochnagar's magnificent mile-long cliff face is seen to advantage from many points along the Deeside road, as are its two conical peaks, which make it the most shapely of the Cairngorm hills. For many, their first acquaintance with the hill comes from ascending the track from the car park at the Spittal of Glenmuick to the summit. Though this route offers pleasant vistas through the pine woods of Allt na Guibhsaich, it is not the finest approach to the hill, which is hidden for most of the way. This is also the day-trippers' route, and you are never out of sight of what can be truly a 'madding crowd'. A day trip is not the best way to get to know Lochnagar, nor any other hill worth knowing well.

Accommodation (of an inferior kind) can be found in Glen Muick, and using this allows for a longer stay, and a more intimate knowledge of Lochnagar.

The Royal Lodge at Allt na Guibhsaich has attached to it a former servants' quarters, converted into a club climbing hut. Access to this is restricted, although an abutting cobbled outhouse used to offer primitive shelter to the unfastidious. And after the ten mile walk from Ballater, those who had not given up at the 'Chuckie Bothy' (a roadman's hut half way up the Glen), would have slept anywhere. Another Royal Lodge lies at Glas allt Shiel, at the west end of Loch Muick, and round the back a door always used to be open for emergency access to a room which gave shelter from the elements, though floor and windows were in poor shape. Behind this doss, a path ascends to the Lochnagar plateau by the Glas Allt waterfall, the finest in the Cairngorms. It is also handy for forays into the majestic Dubh Loch area, the remotest part of the whole Lochnagar massif, and scene of many climbing achievements in the 1960s and 1970s. But neither of these inferior dosses has the quality, charm and wealth of association which belongs to the fabled Gelder Shiel, to which we now turn.

Some years ago, an introduction to the romance of bothying via a trip to the Gelder was in store for a band of unsuspecting novices. They had gathered in the Falkland Cafe in Aberdeen one midweek night, to receive selective invitations, from a band of desperadoes, to participate in their exploits. Those desperadoes had all the aura of myth and fable about them, and seemed as old as the hills themselves, though in retrospect none could have begun their third decade, and their achievements were shrouded in mystery, assumed rather than elaborated. 'We'll meet at the Brig o' Dee, six o'clock on Friday', it was announced.

And at the rallying point on the Friday evening, a large crowd, swollen by rumour and girlfriends, had gathered. Finally the transport arrived, an old beat-up van that was probably older than any of the trio of Che Guevara look-alikes who were in charge of it. The motley crew was downcast at the size and condition of the vehicle. Half of them repaired to the pub, with the promise that the van would return for a second load — a round trip of 100 miles. Meanwhile the rest of the company piled in sacks and other gear, to find that this filled the open back completely. While the leadership climbed in the driving compartment, lesser mortals scrambled on and tried to maintain a hold by grabbing any object — headboard, pack or companion — that looked stable, and the van shuddered westward.

The party who went that night to the Gelder were mainly young proletarian mountaineers, of anarchical political persuasion. Those were the days of YCND and the Vietnam war: weekends not spent scouring the hills would be spent on marches and demonstrations. Taking on the Masters Of War merged into a continuum with taking on the Lairds and their Lackeys, fighting for access to the glens, demolishing hides to give grouse a chance, and sabotaging that ultimate in abominations, the proposed Feshie Road. Few can recall any outsiders using Cairngorm bothies in the 1960's, and most bands shared the composition, if not the politics, of this one — fitters, turners, car mechanics and other skilled artisans, with a sprinkling of upwardly mobile 11-plus successes. Bred on orange juice and the early welfare state, these characters had horizons wider than their forebears.

An exception, in being lower than artisan status, was Fishgut Mac, a real child of the mean streets, from darkest Fittie where pigeon chests and splay toes were endemic. His name was a combination of a tribute to his musical talents (referring to a then popular rock group, Fleetwood Mac) with a reference to his one-time occupation. Mac had worked in a glue factory, boiling up fish guts, heads and tails, and

25

when asked what function this served, would say, 'Fit div ye dae wi' fish heids? Ye haud airoplanes thegither.'

Mac was the archetypical 1960s Woody Guthrie clone, who would come to a doss without his sleeping bag, but never without his guitar. He would while away the evening belting out *A Hard Rain's a Gonna Fall* or a local ballad, such as *The Battle of Harlaw*. Mac's musical taste, and that of his companions, was fairly catholic. Bothy songs, or north-east ballads with innumerable verses, were his favourites, but he also had a fund of Irish rebel songs, hobo ballads and of course the fashionable Dylan added many more to his repertoire.

His sartorial style resembled Dylan or Donovan, rather than a mountaineer, as he strode across the hills in demim jacket and jeans, sporting a peaked cap and a pair of old work boots. Nevertheless, he had enormous strength in his spindly legs, especially when fortified with his favorite meal, a tin each of mince, steak and beans, all in one pot. As with many others, widening horizons increased Mac's discontent with proletarian existence, and he later grafted through nightschool, singing for his supper in local pubs, and eventually became a teacher, a cog in the grey educational machine, '*Eyeless in Gaza, at the mill with slaves*'. The Mac who, on a starlit night on the Ballater road, held the company spellbound with music on the hoof, is no more.

Another character that night was Stumpy, a turner in a local engineering works. His appellation was derived from his size, or lack of it. Though generally a quiet and gentle man, the intellectual of his group, given to inward meditation on the Russian revolution or Metaphysical Poetry, volumes of which protruded from his donkey jacket pockets, he could be driven to fury when a comrade, surveying the starlit heavens would comment, 'Makes you feel small, eh, Stumpy?'

On the other, hand Stumpy was reckoned to be the most sartorially accomplished of the group. Stumpy's old man worked on the trawlers, and had obtained an oilskin designed for Icelandic duty.

With his borrowed oilskin held together by a length of tarry tow, Stumpy resembled Capt. Ahab in search of Moby Dick. He also obtained heavy duty shirts from Polish seamen at the docks, in exchange for hard currency, which the Poles spent on hard drink.

As well as being the acme in terms of dress, Stumpy had a certain aura about him. He'd 'been to the Dolomites', it was said. But that had been in an old banger that took so long to get there that there was only time for starting back. However, Stumpy's intellectual, sartorial and dolomitic stature was marred by his gastronomic deficiences. Indeed, it was opined that his size was due to malnutrition, since he always came away under-provisioned. An apple and some disgusting entrail, like a lung or a heart, was usually his total fare. On a trip with him, you had to take extra provisions, as it was enough to melt the strongest heart to watch Stumpy, with a hangdog look, poking some bleeding organ in his dixie. Stumpy, too, eventually trod the road from the factory floor to the groves of academe, via the mountain path, which offered more to many than did formal education.

That night in the van, while Mac led off with his guitar, and a medley of Irish rebel songs, the company dived into sacks to pillage for gear to keep warm in the freezing night. Out of rucksacks came a weird and wonderful collection of attire, more akin to the contents of a rag and bone merchant's cart, than to present-day climbing dress. Those were the days before the revolution in, and commercialisation of, climbing gear reached the far north-east of Scotland, and when the only source of gear was the scanty display in the back of a money-lender's shop, so lugubrious in furnishings and inmates that it resembled a funeral parlour. Newcomers to the game underwent the hoax of being told it *was* an undertaker's parlour, and were instructed to avoid being measured up, or offered condolences, by saying: 'I've come for the beets: naebody's died'.

Boots apart, (and even here Army and work boots were still widely in evidence in the mid-1960s, sporting the odd tricouni nail in its last stronghold), people made, or made do, with equipment. Mealy Pudding had a set of miner's moleskin trousers that had seen service in the Fife pits: Desperate Dan sported a pair of polisman's breeks, with the bottom of the legs cut off, and one lad covered Shank's pony in a set of second hand jodhpurs. Waterproofs could be anything from cycle tipits, to trawlerman's oilskins, and even plastic bags, but not cagoules. Gaiters there were none, but the leg of an old sock, pulled over boot-tops to prevent some entry of water and stones. The ultra-chic had anoraks, but most preferred donkey jackets or combat jackets.

The sartorial styles were partly due to tbe poverty of youth, allied to traditional Aberdeen parsimony. But partly, also, they were a statement of a political nature: to have been well equipped would have contradicted basic political anarchism.

As the band pulled on their motley clothing they soon resembled a group of IRA men or Castroite guerrillas. At Banchory a policeman dropped his arms, and then his jaw in amazement, as he watched the van approach, a mobile compendium of broken laws. Feeling perhaps that to exercise his legal role would probably cost his life, he chose to exercise discretion instead, and with one hand raised to cover his eyes, waved the band on with the other.

On the van, the novices were regaled by Cuddy, a man who let them into secrets of climbs, dosses, and useful mountain tips. Though he had made it this time, you had begun to notice that Cuddy was rarely there on a Friday night, and instead spent his weekends in the boozers and in bed, as relief from his week's darg in a fish factory. Gradually it became clear that he'd only been away a few times, and even then was generally a hewer of wood and drawer of water, seldom venturing near a hill. But by dint of his listening abilities (posibly due to the efficiency of the organs which earned him his nickname), and his skills as a raconteur, he gained a central position in midweek gatherings devoted to planning future exploits.

In the dark of a starless night, and with the ground covered in snow, the initial destination was reached, and delegating leadership to a partner in crime, the van driver sped back to pick up the reinforcements. The advance party headed off in the direction of Balmoral

Castle, and some of the novices began to suspect that they were to be the innocent accomplices in a daring anti-monarchist exploit. Stumbling about in the pitch darknesss, snow began to fall, and, burdened with unfamiliar packs, they were led along a track which leaves Balmoral behind, and ascends between two cairned hills, until Glen Gelder itself is attained. The party advanced, stragglers bravely trying to keep up, for fear of being stripped and abandoned to the wolves.

Progress was steady till the open moor was reached, and there in a howling wilderness of wind, darkness and spindrift, the path disappeared, and the leaders began to break a trail across the moors. There was much muttering, flashing of torches and consulting of maps, which the novices assumed to be all part of some infallible ritual that would lead them all to shelter. Progress was resumed, and a roaring burn crossed by a footbridge. As one desperado marched on confidently, another whispered hesitantly to him, 'We shouldnae cross a burn, should we?' Pandemonium broke out, and parties threatened to disperse in all directions, though only the leaders had torches and maps. Sounds of sobbing were heard from one lass, which led to a rough 'Fit did ye bring quines for?' Another sat down, and refused to move till prodded and picked up again.

But at this point the leader showed some acumen, realising that if they crossed back over the burn and followed it upstream, it would lead to the vicinity of the bothy. Progress was resumed, and the band assumed that the bothy was near. Following the course of the burn, the struggling party soon all reached the clump of trees which surrounded the shadowy outline of two buildings. One was a modest Royal shooting lodge, the other the bothy. Staggering over the doorstep the party sank down and began to seek out candles to illuminate the gloom. Soon, however, they were easing themselves into sleeping bags, and gaining a fitful sleep, disturbed by the arrival of the other half of the party in the dead of night, much the worse for insobriety.

The band awoke cold, tired and in pain to face the day. Firstly, they examined their lodgings, which brought renewed tears to the eyes of some of the fair sex present — some of them refused to leave their sacks all weekend. For in those days the Gelder Shiel was not the gentrified *pied a terre* that it is today. It was a disused stables, whose floor was cobbled, and over which a stream of water flowed in wet weather, forming a puddle at the doorstep. The window was broken and boarded up, and the only source of light the open door. There was no fire, no tables or chairs of even rude manufacture, and the only softening for the floor was heather roots, which quickly became sodden.

But minds were taken off the surroundings by scenes of great activity, which impressed the apprentice mountaineers. Amid much coiling of ropes and packing of ironmongery, the desperadoes prepared to depart: great deeds were to be done! Off they shot across the moor towards the corrie, to perform acts of heroic grandeur. As the lesser mortals strolled the moor, guddled for fish or tried to strike up relationships with damsels in distress, their thoughts were on whether they could aspire to such epic deeds as were doubtless being done at that moment on the slippery verticals. On their rather early return from the hill, the desperadoes were surrounded by an eager band. What had they done? Evasive and sheepish answers were all that were offered, and some of the more cynical of the novices began to feel that they might not be in the company of latter-day Tom Pateys after all. As the band hirpled homewards on the Sunday, it was divided into those who said 'Never Again!' and those who had contracted an addiction that would last a lifetime.

The Gelder Shiel bothy lies about four miles south of Balmoral, in the glen which gives it its name. It is one of the old shooting lodges that Victoria and Albert had built in the last century. Neither lodge nor stables are used in these days of Land Rovers, but Victoria was made of sterner stuff, and thought nothing of a 25 mile pony trek and overnighting in one of her bothies. Indeed, at the Gelder itself she entertained Eugenie, wife of Napoleon III to a tea of herring grilled in oatmeal. A much later Royal picnic at Gelder led to changes in the bothy which younger users might not be aware of, though it is doubtful if it will figure in the memoirs of Lizzie Regina.

A few years after the expedition just described, a slightly smaller band of mountaineers had made Gelder their base for the weekend. They knew that something was in the air when, on beginning to ascend to Balmoral, a gentleman in a trench coat barred their way, meanwhile fingering inside his lapels to convey the impression he could back up his request. Normally in these circumstances, a quick lecture on Scots law and the absence of a law of trespass accompanied by a determined look, does the trick. In this case it was doubtful whether he would accept this, so the band assured him that their intentions were to head for the high doss in the corrie of Lochnagar, and off the mountain by Glen Muick. To this he agreed, a confrontation was avoided, and progress resumed.

The sequel to this incident came on the Sunday afternoon, when the party was preparing to decamp at the end of the expedition. Suddenly a moving cloud of dust was observed down the glen, and closer observation revealed a convoy of Land Rovers heading towards Gelder. On the side of the bothy, in huge letters, there was a charcoal-emblazoned *Ban Monarchy*, which must have been visible for a considerable distance. The convoy halted, and one vehicle detached itself and came forward, as if to parley. Out of it stepped the same trench coat with its owner again doing his imitation of Napoleon inside its lapels. Behind in the other trucks could be discerned some corgi dogs, complete with their well-known owners.

While most of the party stood their ground, and went about their business, one timid soul fled to the safety of the bothy, to inform Fishgut Mac, busily reheating some gastronomic delicacy, that the Queen had arrived. 'Oh,' came the reply, 'has she got her crown on?' Napoleon informed them that H.M. wanted to have a picnic, and H.M. would therefore be happy if they left.

'Aye, we were jist gyan onywye,' replied a mountaineer. 'Wid she like some spare soup we've left ower for her picnic?'

Napoleon did not deign to reply, but returned to the party to inform them that it was safe to proceed. The Land Rovers arrived and spilled out their occupants. First amongst them was a wee loon later to be famed as Randy Andy, who at that point was more concerned with the pursuit of the corgis with what appeared to be violent rather than amorous, intentions. One of the Ladies of the Chamberpot approached the group of uncouth mountaineers, and peered at their badges through short-sighted eyes.

'Oh, YMCA,'' she said, 'How nice to see young Christian men on the hills.'

'No, wifie, its YCND, ban the bomb. We're nae Christians: we're anarchists.'

On hearing this, the short-sighted eyes opened wide, and she retreated with no further comment to the safety of the monarchist lines. As the royals started their picnic, the mountaineers made their final preparations prior to departure. Through another menial, the Queen offered a lift to one of the party who appeared to have sustained a minor injury. With all eyes on him, though tempted, he refused, knowing it would be seen as a sign of class collaboration he would never outlive. Finally the mountaineers beat an orderly retreat, leaving the royals in possession of the field. One the way down, one of the mountaineers asked: 'We were leaving onywye, but fit wid we hae done if we wernae?'

The band pondered this, till one came up with a reply that seemed to satisfy. 'I dinna ken, but we made oor point onywaye. And that wee detective should be in trouble.'

The outcome of this trip was rather unexpected. A speedy return was made, half expecting to meet opposition to bands of roving republicans. This did not materialise, and the bothy had been gentrified. Bunks had been built, chairs and tables placed there, and the floor concreted, leaving the puddle only a fond memory. A plaque on the wall announced that this was all due to the largesse of Her Majesty.

'I didnae ken she was a jiner tae trade,' quipped Stumpy. But the experience still had to be fitted into the framework of their expectations.

'The *Sunday Post* would say this showed she was a fine wifie, but its aa oor taxes onyway that pyes for this, and that bothy doon the road that she bides in.' That allowed them to use it with a clear conscience, just as they would have had if they had broken into it — as they certainly would have done had it been locked.

The much improved bothy, now maintained by the MBA in these days of straightened Royal finances, is still open to all comers and still offers the best access to the corrie of Lochnagar. A fine, safe walk that really gets the newcomer right into the heart of some of the finest cliff scenery in Britain, is to ascend from the Gelder to the loch in the corrie, and to skirt this till the foot of the Black Spout is reached. This is an easy scree rake, that leads through the rock architecture of Lochnagar, to the summit plateau, and gives no problem, except in a really heavy build up of snow in winter. The more adventurous pedestrian can ascend by forking off at the left-hand branch of the Black Spout. This involves a negotiation of the huge chokestone which blocks it, a tight and messy business, especially when the hill is running with water. At the top of this route is another alternative, the couthily named Crumblin Cranny, which seems to disintegrate as it is ascended, and requires a little care.

Mention of the corrie of Lochnagar leads to its famous howff, perched high above the loch, and below the towering cliffs behind. It lies in an unrivalled location

> *under a boulder situated on the corrie side of the ridge falling from the summit plateau to Glen Gelder, some 200 feet above the innermost of the ink-blot lochans formed at the outlet to the main loch.'* SMC Guide to the Cairngorms, 1962, Vol.2. P. 7.

In fine weather, nothing can beat an overnight stay in the howff, whose main attraction lies in its supreme remoteness, in which you can enjoy the peace of the mountain when other men have gone, and only the deer and eagles remain.

Using the howff as a base, it is possible to complete several climbs in a weekend, and from it, in the dark days of one-inch-to-the-mile maps and red-covered SMC guides, a trio of mountaineers emerged one morning, intent on organising expeditions onto the rocks in pursuit of adventure and glory. Trekking upwards to the foot of Gargoyle Direct, they each in turn performed the climbers' traditional ecological action at the terrace at the foot of the climb, an action that has its source in sheer terror. The party was composed of an enthusiastic, a lukewarm and a distinctly reluctant member. When the first two discovered that the latter was unable to tie knots, he was man-handled onto the rope, and left to fend for himself as the hindmost of the party. Waiting for the others to ascend, he studied the luxuriant growth of the terrace, and understood that many others had been moved to fear where he now stood.

They left the terrace, and moved up a groove to a ledge, where the leader — Desperate Dan himself — made his first halt. The next section led to a cave below a chokestone, and the first man took the crux, a 20 foot pitch on the wall to the right, in fine style. Moving up a chimney to a platform, he placed a running belay *en route*. The second and third arrived thereafter, with a bit of unorthodox arse and elbow technique, and much humphing. Next they gained a tower, behind which the grim outline of the gargoyle itself, like some fiendish Gothic monster, could be seen on the horizon. From the amphitheatre below the gargoyle, an easy route slants right, but it is messy. The leader's blood was up, and his appendages were dragged up the V. Diff. finish, by a strenuous chimney. On the plateau, their delight knew no bounds — their first V. Diff., and one that was well-known, too!

'Gie's the runner, and we'll ging doun tae the next ane,' demanded Dan. Runners are removed by the last man, as any text book will tell you. But the last man had not read the text books, leaving all instruction and responsibility to his companions. Slowly it sank in that he had committed a *faux pas*. His naive idea that the wee lengths of wire with a nut attached were expendible began to fade. 'I left it there. I couldnae get it oot.'

We spare the reader the expostulations which greeted this piece of news, but it was a somewhat chastened party that moved off towards the Black Spout, down which they descended to the foot of their next target, the Stack.

The leader zig-zagged up the slabs to the foot of the wall, followed by his second — who was no other than the luke-warm Stumpy. The wall was designated mild severe without a shoulder. Attempts to balance on that of the second led to great totterings and staggerings, and the unfortunate was finally squatted on all-fours, while the vibramed soles of his leader traced elaborate designs on his back. Finally, however, he managed to drag himself up to the large grassy platform which divides the upper from the lower section of the climb, and his accomplices followed. The next section begins with a chimney, which is blocked by boulders near the top, and turned by a 30 ft. traverse on the left. On a traverse, runners are essential, as a slip will lead not only to a fall, but to a wild swing. The first two men crossed, and the third, the culprit of the Gargoyle, arrived at the beginning of the traverse. Instead of reassuringly following the line of the climb, the rope swung freely across the chasm.

The runner had been removed.

To this day he is unsure whether it was an oversight, as his second later claimed, or a punishment, to make him realise that gear is worth its weight in gold. But there was nothing for it, and he began to inch his way across the ledge, which fortunately had convenient hand holds above, and he reached the next belay point in some trepidation.

'It's a good job ye didnae faa,' was the greeting he received from Dan. 'Ye wouldna even hae stotted.'

The rest of the climb, a series of chimneys, was completed in silence. And with mingled, unspoken feelings, they again headed down the Black Spout and towards the howff in the gloaming. But as the cliff was left behind the realisation sank in that that two of the better climbs on it had been done, and by the time they reached the howff they were all convinced that they were apprentices in the rocky arts no longer. Yet there was still only one amongst them who could tie more than the simplest knot. Like many others, luck spared them from the possible consequences of their foolhardiness.

For those who do not aspire to climb, Gelder Shiel offers many shorter day walks that explore the foothills of Lochnagar. A fine walk is to cross the shoulder of the great mountain, and head for the Sandy Loch, lonely and remote beneath the Stuic, which offers a fine but easy scramble to the plateau. Shallow, the loch heats up quickly on a sunny day, and a pleasant bathe can be had after a hard day on the hill. An alternative is to descend the glen for a mile or so, and fork west into the rocky pine-clad hills of the Ballochbuie forest, a wonderland to explore on a fine day, with the rocks glinting through the pines.

Further down Glen Gelder, if you keep to the old path by the burn and not the Land Rover track, there lies the ruins of a clachan, with a quite distinct street pattern. Like the rest of Deeside, this area was extensively cleared from the mid-18th century. On a grassy knoll beside the clachan you can get a clear view to the corrie, and a realisation that what is now a wilderness was not always so, but was made thus, for greed and profit. , And today the descendants of those who evicted the people, and destroyed the forests to turn the land to hunting, talk of 'protecting the wilderness',which means keeping it for themselves.

The absence of a fire in Gelder meant that, summer and winter, an early retreat to sleeping bags was essential. Time was whittled away reading the inscriptions on the wall. *East, West, Gelder's best* repeated musingly was like counting sheep. Marathon card, domino or chess games, until fatigue took over, were an alternative. But the gloomy atmosphere of Gelder, especially before it was upgraded, encouraged feelings of a supernatural nature, and made story telling a popular pastime. Possibly the proximity of Lochnagar, with its fair share of climbing fatalities, also encouraged this. Tales were told in the mid-1960s that Gelder was originally opened because two exhausted climbers had collapsed and died outside its locked door. Whether these or similar stories were true or not, they offered fertile ground for those with inventive imaginations.

One one occasion a lone climber in Gelder prepared to turn in for the night. After carefully barring the door, he bedded down and extinguished the candle. Nothing could be heard but the soughing of the wind in the pines. Until, softly, at first, then louder, footsteps were heard approaching the door. The inmate of the bothy, recalling that the ghosts of the two perished climbers were reputed to try and gain entry on the anniversary of their ordeal, leaped up and cried 'Who's there?'

He had no doubt that he was witnessing the unleashing of unholy forces, as he heard a scratch, scratch at the door. As this become more insistent, he ran to the door and battered on it with his ice axe. The noise stopped and the shaken climber made his way back to bed. But then the scratching began even more loudly, and what he had taken for the wind sounded ever more like a human — or inhuman — moan. Fear inspired courage, and taking a torch in one hand and the axe in the other, the victim of ghoulish persecution swung back the door — just in time to see a magnificent stag disappearing into the trees. Its antlers had been what he had taken for the nails of the ghost.

This story was retold many times by older hands in Gelder. As one would tell of the mysterious scratchings, another would slip out to contribute noises off, drop from the rafters, or burst open the door at points of tension, to reduce novices to quivering masses of jelly.

But lighter tales would be told, too, a favourite here was that concerning two characters who succumbed to temptation on a night of pouring rain at Allt na Guibhsaich. Persuading a window to be open, they laid out their sacks in the kitchen and went to sleep. But soon the noise of an engine ended their repose. Keys rattled in the lock and torches flashed.

'Just act deid', said one of the malefactors, and vanished into the depths of his sack. For want of an alternative, his companion did likewise.

The *bona fide* group entered to find the intruders. 'There's somebody here,' said one of them, more observant than the rest. As the bodies refused to stir, the new entrants were at a loss what action to take. Those in the sacks heard sounds of unpacking and the preparation of refreshments, but little talk. Still the intruders lay inert; any communication would have to contain an admission of guilt, and had to be avoided. Eventually footsteps were heard, indicating that the recent entrants were heading upstairs to bed.

'Fit div we dae noo?'

'Ging tae sleep!' replied the other, and rolled over.

In the morning the intruders arose early, packing quickly. Though sounds could be heard upstairs, no-one descended. They vacated the bothy, half expecting to be pursued, but the out-psyching of the *bona fide* occupants by the two autistic figures seemed to be complete. On the path to Lochnagar the companions were mighty pleased with themselves, and chuckled at their coup. Though damage was the ultimate sin, the anarchic figures of that period regarded locked huts as a privilege that it was justifiable to attack. *Oh for doors to be open, and invite with gilded edges*, was how they, like the beggars in Auden's poem thought things should be. And this time dreams had come true.

Possibly because of its ease of access, Gelder Shiel was always a gang doss, where big parties went, and the incidents came fast and furious. As numbers were whittled down, it tended to lose its popularity to other, more austere, howffs. Much of those apprentice years in Gelder, below the most beautiful of the Cairngorm hills, was mis-spent in idling, but it was not wasted. In retrospect it is possible to see that despite what the years have added in experience, technique and confidence, there has been something lost — the cameraderie, the expectation of adventure, the sheer delight of bothy life, to which the mountain was often a secondary appendage, an afterthought, a footnote — all these have waned with the passing of time.

A WEEKEND ACROSS COUNTRY

After leaving Glasgow's Queen Street station, the north-bound train trundles its way through the innards of the city before emerging into industrial suburbia — through Clydebank and Dalmuir and then on to Bowling and Dumbarton. It soon leaves urban Strathclyde, to run through the genteel estuary towns of the Gairloch before reaching the first mountain pass of the day's journey. At the summit, Whistlefield. Is it imagination, or did the old steam trains really scream shrilly with delight at their day's first triumph? Today, such reminiscences seem out of place. The giant diesels lack such romance, and slide down unannounced to the nuclear-bunkered slope above Loch Long. At Arrochar the train will change direction — and lochs — by slithering through a gap in the mountains to Loch Lomond. After the long slow curves above this famous water comes the junction at Crianlarich, hard-won by a steep, squealing, grinding climb through wild Glen Falloch. Then on again with a quicker pace across easier ground to Tyndrum, famous for its two stations. At the upper station, the Fort William train will catch its breath before curves and huge viaducts will aid its circumvention of Auch, below the cone of Beinn Dorain.

After the halt at Bridge of Orchy, there is a dramatic change. Until now, the journey has been circuitous. The train has clung to lochside and hill on rails seldom straight. But now, coming round the lower reaches of Ben Dotaidh, the track uncoils itself, and the mountainous terrain becomes suddenly diminished as it is replaced by a new and incredible beauty. In one's mind flatness is often associated with dullness, but the Rannoch Moor, though certainly flat, presents passengers with a unique and exciting prospect, for as the train passes

Ben Alder Cottage

through the pine forest above Achallater, they cannot fail to be struck by this wild place, populated only by a handful of people and herds of red deer. This is a genuine wilderness, and travellers who cross it by train will be rewarded with intriguing sights denied to road-users.

For most passengers, the strange, old-fashioned stations that materialise, often out of thick mist, and seem to serve no community, are merely quaint diversions on their journey to the north. However, to the mountaineer and hillwalker, these halts give access to isolated bothies located on the fringes of the moor. Unfortunately for the weekender (who usually had to be back at his work on Monday morning) there was no Sunday train service, so it could not be used for the return journey. Escape could only be achieved by walking out and hitch-hiking home.

This is the story of a typical weekend for some Glasgow climbers who used such places in search of a bit of out-of-season exercise and adventure.

The decision would be made over pints in the Red Lion, some Wednesday night in late November. Ben Alder cottage was to be the target for Saturday night. They would hitch-hike to Bridge of Orchy on Friday night and catch the early train on Saturday morning. It was too expensive to catch the train in Glasgow, and Bridge of Orchy was the point of departure of rail from road. They would take the train to Rannoch station. From there it is only six or seven miles to the cottage beside Loch Ericht, so there would be time that day to climb Ben Alder. They'd take in wine, have a big fire and a sing-song before leaving the next morning to walk up the loch shore to Dalwhinnie. There would be time for a drum-up there before hitch-hiking back down to Glasgow via Perth.

Of the four young faces round the table, only Jimmy's registered anything less than enthusiasm for the project. He was not sure about this off-season hillwalking indulged in by some of the lads in order to keep fit in that blank period between the end of the rock climbing season and the beginning of the snow and ice climbing. He was, after all, a big-time climber, a member of the Creagh Dhu, and he knew

41

these hillwalkers were a bit soft — didn't they wear those daft woolly hats with a pom-pom sewn on the top? No, he was reluctant to join in such a dubious activity. He'd have to be persuaded. This he eventually was, with promises of rare and wild delights and of comfortable bothies with roaring fires.

As Balloch was considered to be the best place for hitch-hiking north, the four made their way there the following Friday night. Ignoring the temptations of the pubs and dancing, they walked up to the junction at the garage where the old road north used to pass. By the early sixties, the hitch-hiking of the regulars was a well-organised affair, quite unlike that described by Borthwick, where desperate and competitive characters vied with each other by hiding in the woods in order to get the first chance of a lift.

As Borthwick notes, hitch-hiking in those circumstances:
'....Becomes a battle of wits, based on the good biblical truth that the last shall be first and the first shall be last. It must be so, for one immutable rule in competitive hitch-hiking is that the last man gets the first hitch: on any road, the man who lags furthest behind is the first to be overtaken by passing traffic, and therefore has the advantage over any more energetic souls who may have walked on ahead.' (1969, P.72)

Internecine warfare of this sort was avoided in the sixties by two simple and civilised arrangements. Firstly, you didn't walk along the road. You stayed put in a good spot that would allow space for the obliging drivers to pull off the road. Staying put has the added advantage of giving the impression that you could not walk to wherever you were going. The second simple expedient was that while one guy stood out on the road hitching, the others would stay out of sight behind any cover that was available. At Balloch there would be up to sixteen hopefuls hiding behind the old garage, waiting for their turn and passing the time by recounting stories about epic hitch-hikes. If the active hitch-hiker got someone to stop, he would assess the space available in the vehicle, and ask the driver if he could take his mate as well.   In this,way, given luck, the queue would quickly diminish.

On the Friday night in question, luck was absent.   It was dark and cold, and deep snow lay on the ground.   Worse than this, no-one seemed keen to stop.   Behind the garage, out of sight of the passing traffic, a dozen or so hopefuls were trying to ignore the cold.   Some jogged up and down, others beat their arms across their chests, their breath condensed in billowing clouds on the freezing air.   However, no matter what their activity, they were listening to those who stood telling tales, in quiet voices, of other nights and days spent on the road.   One told of the longest lift he ever had, when he hitched a ride in a big Mercedes from just outside London all the way to Istanbul. At the other end of the spectrum of luck, another told how it took him a week to hitch-hike from Skye to Glencoe.   But the story that amused the most was of the short trip from Tarbet, Loch Lomond, to Balloch, a distance of only twenty-odd miles.

The man who told it reported how on one wet Sunday night in summer he was standing outside the hotel at Tarbet hitching to Glasgow when he was approached by a very drunken tinker, who had a proposition.   Push his old van to get it started, and he would give the hiker a lift as far as Balloch.   The hiker thought quickly.   The tinker was very drunk, his van very old and decrepit, but the hiker had been there for hours, and the midges were bad.   So he decided to take a chance, hoping that the van would not go fast enough to kill them if they had an accident.

The deal was sealed with a handshake and a slap on the back.   The hiker threw his pack into the rear of the van, where, among the jumble of old clothes and rusty tools reclined a set of well-used bagpipes, and a very doleful-looking whippet.   Later the hiker was to learn that the tinker was an early exponent of what has become a common commercial sight and sound beside many a Scottish beauty spot — the roadside piper who plays *Scotland the Brave*, all the while posing for the tourists' photographs.   This one, however, lacked the resplendent uniform that appears to be *de rigeur* today.

43

The hiker was correct about the inability of the van to travel at speed, for it barely managed a trundle. And just as well, because the tinker was an avid talker who believed in eye-to-eye contact with his listener, as well as the use of his hands to emphasise his points. Thus the van lurched from side to side as the driver, immersed in some incoherent monologue, rather absentmindedly negotiated the infamously difficult road.

After a short while they reached an hotel where they stopped while the tinker tried to convince his passenger that it would be a fine Christian act if he would take the driver into the pub for a good pint of Scottish ale. Considering the state of inebriation exhibited by that gentleman, the hiker, at first felt disinclined to help reduce his chances of reaching Balloch in one piece. However, not only was the tinker persuasive, he himself felt rather thirsty. What the hell, he thought, it's supposed to be an adventure. Let's live dangerously!

They did not receive a warm Highland welcome from the owner of the establishment, who, while pulling the ordered pints, eyed the tinker with a great deal of suspicion. He had some reason, for the tinker proved a noisy and difficult customer. He was shuffling round, back hunched, arms held aloft in some grotesque parody of a Highland dance. Snatches of loud, but incomprehensible monologues were punctuated by strange tuneless songs, sung in a language that might have been English or Gaelic. The rest of the clientele may have looked puzzled or uneasy, but the tinker was enjoying himself, and cried for more ale. His passenger, rather perversely enjoying the owner's disquiet, agreed and up to the bar he strode.

The owner, his greed for profit overcoming his dislike of the tinker, pulled the beer, all the time glowering at the cavorting, capering figure. When he pushed the glasses towards the hiker, he bent his head in a gesture that indicated he wanted the man to come close for a word. 'Get that dirty wee mink out of here as quick as you can,' he hissed through clenched teeth. It was the wrong thing to say, for the hiker, being a democrat, believed in the equality of all men before the bar. Hence, he drank his beer even more slowly, allowing the tinker to become even more boisterous.

Eventually the tinker finished his beer, and immediately set about trying to extract more from his passenger. Alas, his companion informed him he only had the price of his train fare from Balloch to Glasgow left. The tinker was disappointed, but not dismayed. He had a plan. 'Ah'll get the pipes oot and gie them *Scotland the Brave*, and you can bottle the punters for a few boab.' And without waiting for an answer he fetched his pipes from the van.

The noise was horrendous. Being so drunk, the tinker could hardly stand, never mind co-ordinate his fingers to produce something that resembled a tune. The other customers recoiled in horror. Outside, the whippet began to howl in competition. The owner, no lover of the pipes, was beside himself with rage, and he indicated with rude gestures that the tinker should leave. He, however, with his eyes tightly closed in a grotesque effort to co-ordinate sodden mind with hapless fingers, was oblivious to the chaos he was causing. Suddenly, with an exasperated gesture, the owner disappeared only to return a few minutes later in the company of some husky young men. They descended on the tinker and clasping their hands to him, sped him out of the pub. The door slammed as the pipes gave a last deflated wail. The young men turned their attention to the hiker, who, realising that his short trip into the world of showbiz was rapidly coming to an end, raised his hands in a gesture of goodwill and peace, only to find himself hurtling out of the door to join his musical partner.

Despite the tinker's pleadings that they should try the bagpipe ploy at every inn they came to, the hiker resisted and the journey passed off without further incident. It came to an abrupt end at Balloch, just outside the police station, when suddenly the van, not the most silent of vehicles, began to make a sound akin to a regiment of tanks hurtling down a cobbled street. Its exhaust had given up the unequal task of hanging on by a few strips of rusty metal. Without bothering to pull the van over to the side of the road, the tinker stopped and immediately slid under the chassis to appraise the extent of the damage.

The van was almost instantly surrounded by a small crowd of damp daytrippers, who thought there was the prospect of some entertainment to brighten up their wet Sunday.   Some passed out spurious advice, while others made laboured comments about the van's fitness to take part in sporting events.   'Ah didny ken there was a rally passin' through the day,' was typical of the attempts at wit.

The hiker also alighted from the van and looked nervously through the crowd towards the police station.   Right enough, there were two policemen at the window straining their necks to see what was going on.

'Gie us some o' that wire oot the back o' the van.'   The tinker's request distracted the hiker's attention away from the police, and he began to rummage around the back of the vehicle.   Minutes later, just when he was about to hand the tinker the wire, he felt someone take a grip of his shoulder.   It was, of course, the police.   'What's your part in this, son?'   'Me?   A'm jist a hitch-hiker.'

'On yer way, then.'

'What aboot him?'

'We'll see to him, and it'll no be for the first time.   So on yer way, or you'll get liftit as well.'

So, feeling more than a bit guilty at leaving the tinker to his fate, the hiker collected his pack and slunk off for the train.

The story had served as a useful diversion from the boredom of waiting, but as it came to an end the listeners once again became aware of the cold that crept up through the soles of their boots and into the marrow of their bones.   The lights of the Loch Lomond Hotel became very attractive.   In low murmurs seductive voices began to weaken the impoverished resolve of cold-stiffened minds, and some began to think of spending slender pecuniary resources on the winter hitch-hikers' friend — a fur coat.   It would be a mistake on the part of a naive reader to imagine that the hotel sold cheap articles of furry clothing, for what is being referred to here is a particularly virulent cocktail of strong beers: a Fowlers Wee Heavy and a Carlsburg Special Lager. This brew did not keep the hitch-hiker warm, but it numbed his brain, thus serving for him a similar reality-blocking function as do coca leaves for Bolivian tin miners. Its name comes from the texture of the tongue after an over-indulgence in such refreshment.

The debate between temptation on the one hand and puritanical suffering on the other was resolved by the arrival of an open-back lorry. It was going to Mallaig to pick up fish, and it would take everybody. There was a mad flurry of packs and legs as people climbed up onto the evil-smelling back of the lorry, there to crouch through the endless night in the deepest of cold. An hour and a half of frozen torture on heaving boards that threatened to cast people into the rushing inky darkness brought the relief of the Bridge of Orchy. Although the temperature was way below freezing, the four friends felt warm after their desperate journey. 'That was like riding a bucking bronco in a wind tunnel in Alaska,' shouted Kenny to the frozen figures who still had many miles to go that night. His attempt at wit earned him a few weak smiles among the muted and muffled sound of parting farewells and good lucks.

In the deep silence of the kind only experienced in snow-bound winter nights the lads set about solving the problem of finding a doss for the night. This was the only part of their plan not fully thought out, for they did not know of any regularly available shelter in this hamlet. However, they spotted a wee cottage next to the hotel and beside it there was a wooden barn. A hesitant knock on the cottage door was rewarded by the response of a frail and frightened female voice, that sounded as if it came from deep inside a bed which was even deeper inside an an ancient bed-recess.

What did they want? 'Can we sleep in your barn tonight, missus?' The answer was in the affirmative, so the lads crunched off through the frozen snow. The door was not locked. They pushed it open and stumbled into the darkness, to find what looked like a scene from the nativity.   In one stall there was a donkey, in another there were some calves, there were even some sheep.   Packs were dropped onto the floor and spaces prepared in the straw for sleeping.   Accompanying all this activity was the inevitable banter.

'See if Joseph and Mary are in the back there.'

'Did you remember the frankincense?   Whit aboot the myrrh? Did ye no get it when ye were in yon myrrh shoapp?

'Is this the right place?   Ah didnae see the big star.'

And so on and so on.   Only with this topic exhausted did they finally fall asleep.

In the morning they were up early.   The train got in around seven, and they wanted to cook their breakfast in the waiting room before it arrived.   This they achieved, and soon they were on their way, warmed by their feast of porridge and excited by the prospect of adventure.   They stared out at the desolate white wastes beyond the train windows.   There were the inevitable herds of red deer, thin and hungry-looking, and slowed by the cold so that they took only passing interest in the train.   Perhaps they had noticed the darkening sky, now with clouds almost purple in hue, and were awaiting with silent stoicism winter's next terrible onslaught.

The scene at Rannoch Station could have been taken straight from the pages of *Doctor Zhivago*.   The porter, clad in a heavy ankle-length coat and woollen balaclava, shouted out the name of the station, his breath issuing from underneath his walrus moustache in great clouds that hung in the still air around his head.   Everywhere there was fresh, deep snow, wind-blown into every cranny of the exposed station.   It stuck to windows and made the wooden benches look like big, fat, comfortable sofas.   It even managed to obliterate the large blue sign that announced the name of this British Railways' outpost.

The lads did not hang around, and as soon as they had shouldered their packs they stepped out into the unmarked whiteness.   The sky was getting darker, and the faint rustle of a north-east wind could have been detected by the meteorologically aware. The signs of the impending storm, however, failed to breach a consciousness braced by youthful enthusiasm, and occupied by the problem of finding the start of the path that would lead them onto the high moor they had to traverse to reach the bothy.

They had not gone far on that moor when the storm broke. At first, in terms of snow and wind, it was not too bad. The real problem at that time was walking in the correct direction. People who have lived their lives in the city will find it difficult to imagine the sensory deprivation experienced by someone walking in white mist on snow covered ground. There is no horizon, no difference between air and ground, and every step becomes a lottery. On top of a mountain this can be very dangerous, for without careful navigation there is a risk of walking over a cliff. The boys knew this. What they learned that day was that such weather conditions could also be very dangerous on flat moors, for very soon they were heading away from their destination in completely the wrong direction. They were saved from walking off into the nowhere western wilderness of the Rannoch Moor by a brief lifting of the clouds, which revealed a collection of small lochs that were not on their orginal route.

Thus chastened, one of their number pulled a compass from his pack and took a bearing for Loch Ericht. With some relief the lads continued on their way. They had not gone far, however, when there was a further deterioration in the weather. Now accompanying the white blankness came heavy snowfall and a fearful, gusting wind.

Those lads were fit, yet they quickly realised their reserves of stamina and strength were being drained by the difficulties they faced. They were walking straight into the gale and the blinding snow, but that was not their main problem. The rough terrain on which they walked was covered by knee-deep snow that often hid drifts which were chest high. In such conditions the miles won were exhausting, and seemed to go on for ever. What was meant to be a quick and easy dander across the moor, a prelude to their ascent of Ben Alder, had now become a terrible struggle. Their earlier enthusiasm had long since fled and it looked as if it was going to be joined by deserting confidence. Into the space vacated in the mind by that bold emotion crept a new and uneasy feeling. Memories stirred. Was it not just to the north of here that in 1951 a party of four men and one woman had been caught in a bad storm while making their way to Ben Alder cottage. The four men had died of exhaustion in the driving snow, but the woman had miraculously survived. 'None of us are lassies,' was the grim thought of the compass bearer as he floundered yet again in a deep snow drift.

It was soon after that the worst happened. The man in front, mind occupied with leading the desperate progress, heard through the ear-blocking wind the cries of his companions urging him to stop. He turned round to see Jimmy lying in the snow shaking his head. A few reverse steps brought him into a conversation that made him shudder. Jimmy was doing his Capt. Oates bit.

'Ah cannae go oan, boays. Just leave me. Ah'll make it masel,' he moaned.

His three companions looked at each other. This was not good news. True, they were not that far from safety, but a few miles in this weather was turning out to be a very difficult proposition. If they had been older and wiser they may have turned around and with the help of the wind retreated back to the station. But they were neither older nor wiser, and even if the thought of retreat had passed through their heads, it probably would have been dismissed because there was no bothy for them there. They had to go on, but what were they going to do with Jimmy?

No doubt it must have gone through at least one mind, 'We'll do our Capt. Scott to his Oates and leave him.' But if anyone thought this, it went unspoken. It was Alistair who solved the problem. He walked up to the prostrate figure and kicked him, a short, sharp kick.

'Get up, you bastard. You're gonnae die if you lie there.' It took a few more kicks to persuade Jimmy that this might indeed be the case. Reluctantly he got up. He did not look good, but at least he was on his feet and with the consumption of a few frozen Mars Bars the crisis seemed to be over.

Shortly after, as if to confirm this, the weather changed. The snow stopped and the cloud lifted, leaving a supernaturally blue sky. The going was still difficult. The wind still blew and they still had to contend with the lousy conditions underfoot. But now at least they could see where they were going, and this inevitably raised spirits. There was the loch, and to the left the woods. Beyond the woods, by about a quarter of a mile, the cottage lay. Soon they would have a fire going and some hot food inside them. That was what they thought, but it was not going to be as easy as that.

Alistair was first to confront the problem. In the final mile he had pulled ahead of his companions, and as a consequence he reached the cottage first. It was occupied in strength by a University mountaineering club, and their leader was saying something that Alistair never thought he would hear in an open bothy.

'The cottage is full. You can't get in.'

'Full? Ah can't get in,' repeated Al incredulously. They were miles from anywhere, in the well-advanced afternoon of a short winter's day. They had just come through a nasty storm. They were wet and cold, and this bum was telling him that he could not get into an open doss. What had happened to all that camaraderie of the mountains he had heard and read about?

At this point the others arrived and on noticing the tension in the room, asked Al what was wrong. He told them. Jimmy reacted quickly and dramatically. He dropped his pack and announced that he was going to do battle. Only a couple of hours earlier, high on the moor, he looked as if he was going to become a statistic in the Scottish Mountaineering Club's accident report, but Jimmy was a street-fighting man from Possil, and no-one, least of all this posh twit, was going to keep him out of this bothy.

He was advancing menacingly on the inhospitable spokesman when he was restrained by his companions. There was no problem, they reassured him. There was simply no place they could go. They were staying. Fixing a severe eye on the students, Al bent down and moved some sleeping bags to one side.

'There's room here,' he said.

It was the students' move: they they did not make it. The second crisis of the day was over.

This incident illustrated very clearly the different attitudes and philosophies found among hill users and, because of this lack of congruence, it can be argued that the so-called camaraderie of the hills is a bit of a myth. Most people are conservative enough to want the bothy to themselves. It is part of that British reserve that made people hunt for empty compartments on trains, when trains had compartments. Despite that, most will tolerate the presence of others, especially if they're people they know. Some, like the students, can be downright mean and will try to claim proprietorial rights. This was something the lads were going to experience another time in the same cottage.

In that case the lads were installed in the best room of the two-roomed house when a party from the Loch Rannoch private school arrived through the cold twilight of a Saturday afternoon. The master in charge came into the room where the lads were just beginning to cook their evening meal. He ignored their invitation to a drop of tea or a wee dram from the bottles, and proceeded, in hostile tones, to question their right to be there. 'Colonel So-and-so (the laird) said no-one would be here this weekend,' he informed his now totally indifferent audience. 'I know,' said one of them flatly, 'People come over here without even asking for permission. It's really bloody diabolical.' Sensing he was getting a rise taken out of him, the master retreated to his charges in the other room, there, no doubt, to fume silently over the impudence of the lower orders.

The source of this conflict seems to lie in the clash of two different and opposing cultures. The students and the teacher represented the world from which some of the lads were escaping when they sought the freedom of the hills. There, for two whole days they were out of the control of the bosses, and clocking on and all the rest of the rules and regulations. The students were a bunch of la-di-da softies who represented a world of privilege denied to them, and one day they (the students) would be the bosses. The teacher, well, he had already been their boss. They were familiar with his methods and they had little cause to like them.

Then there was the problem of the different approaches to hills and climbing. In very general terms the middle class outlook is very utilitarian. Bothies are to be used as bases for climbing and hillwalks. This means travelling light and spending the short winter's day trying to achieve something, which in turn means there is little or no alcohol carried and no time to collect firewood to cheer up the long night. As a consequence of this serious approach there is not much hilarity in such parties, for they are off to their beds very early in the evening. Even during their waking hours they tend to be very quiet and reserved. This seems to concern some of them, for reports have it that a very famous hillwalker of this ilk (a man who has recently published a book on his greatest exploits), was seen in a bothy, where he said little to his companions, and nothing to strangers, reading a book whose contents were devoted to the improvement of conversational ability!

In contrast to this, the working class approach, once again in very general terms, tends towards the hedonistic. Alcohol is nearly always carried and if there was a choice between going up some big, windy and wet hill in zero visibiility and collecting wood for the night, then the latter was nearly always chosen. Moreover, they tended to be quite noisy and garrrulous. A man could gain status if he had a good collection of stories to tell round the fire. Finally, they like a good sing-song, favouring not only Scots and Irish folk songs, but also those American ones about drifters and railroad engineeers.

Perhaps this is what lay at the root of the inhospitable welcome the lads received from the students. They represented a major threat of disturbance to the students' tranquillity. For the lads' part, they thought it was strange that here was a bunch of people whose plans to climb had been obliterated by the recent storm, yet who nevertheless seemed content to sit, cold and miserable in a fireless bothy. They'd soon change that. After a cup of tea they'd retrace their steps to the wood to collect fuel for the night's jollifications.

The two sides co-existed uneasily that night. The lads round a roaring fire, glasses filled with wine, singing songs and telling stories. The students were surly, silent in the dancing shadow background, no doubt wishing they could get some sleep. Of course, not all the students were hostile. Some, beginners no doubt, unskilled at interpreting the subtle nuances of social separation, joined the group round the fire. They had never seen anything like the style of these representatives of the western proletariat, so, oblivious to the glowering looks of their colleagues, they accepted drinks from the proffered bottles and listened to the telling of the tales and fables.

One subject inevitably touched upon was ghosts. Ben Alder cottage was supposed to be haunted. It was claimed that the last resident, depressed by the isolation and bad weather, hanged himself from a meathook that could still be seen in the ceiling of one of the rooms. The Ben Alder ghost, however, like many other ghosts, has proved difficult to verify. Everybody has heard of it, but nobody has actually seen or heard it. Everybody, however, seems to know somebody who has seen the ghost. In this way, myth has become reality, for in fact there is probably no ghost in the cottage, and if there is, it is not that of the last occupant. It has been ascertained on no less an authority than that of the warden of the hostel at Loch Ossian, that the last occupant walked out on his own two feet, happy no doubt to be away from the uneven struggle of earning a living in such a difficult place. Still, the cottage *is* creepy and isolated, so it is easy to imagine that some lonely or sensitive souls, out there during a windswept night, could think they heard or saw an unaccounted-for presence.

Also discussed that night was the question of the existence or not of Clunie's Cage. According to Robert Louis Stevenson in his book *Kidnapped*, this was some kind of structure built round a cave in which Bonnie Prince Charlie took refuge during his escape from Culloden to the Western Isles.   Like the ghost, the existence of the cave has been difficult to verify.   While some claim it was located in a collection of boulders above the cottage, others think it was to be found in the corrie of Ben Alder.   This, of course, mattered little to the now diminished group round the fire.   They were young and full of romance and excitement.   Ghosts existed and they were following in the footsteps of Charlie, albeit in reverse.

The cold dawn of the next day fetched in a reality that cleared minds of drink and romance.   The weather was not good, and they still had to walk the fourteen or so miles to Dalwhinnie before beginning the wearisome hitch-hiking down to Glasgow.   Soon they were moving slowly, heads down into bitter snow squalls.

The going was not as difficult as the previous day, yet it was late afternoon when they arrived at the deserted station of Dalwhinnie. The weather had again changed.   The wind had dropped and the cloud rolled back to reveal a lead-blue sky, tinged with the rose of the dying day.   The early evening stars showed themselves discreetly and the temperature dropped steadily.

The drum-up on the empty platform was taken at a leisurely pace.   This was one of the great pleasures of the weekend — the outdoor repast enjoyed even in deep winter.   Moreover, there was a reluctance to hurry to the long and dreary hitch-hike home.   So they lingered, hunched down round their paraffin stoves, hands clasped round their mugs of tea, murmuring in low voices, picking over the bones of their weekend.   'Some storm that.'   'What d'ye mek o' that mug tryin' to keep us oot o' the doss?   Someboddy'll stick it on him wan day, so they wull.'   'Aye, right enuff, so they wull.'

Eventually, when time and cold meant they could linger no longer, they made their way, stiff-jointed to the road, and while three hid in the woods, one, deemed lucky by some undeclared process, pointed his thumb south to the intermittent traffic.   In this way it came to an end.   In fits and starts down the A9 and through Perth.   One twosome leap-frogging the other.   Down through the darkness and the cold to Glasgow and Monday and work. The promise of the weekend had been fulfilled. It had all been there: adventure, and laughs, beauty and romance. They would do it again. Most of them, that is, for on the following Wednesday, Jimmy revealed an astonishingly short memory when it was suggested that he should join a similar expedition.

'Ach, Ah've shown Ah can dae that. There's no point in doin' it again.'

The strange thing about Jimmy was that he did not seem to understand why everybody fell about laughing.

BOTHIES FABLED

Few bothies are known by name to non-bothiers, but the most likely candidates for this honour lie in the northern Cairngorms area. Corrour Bothy, Landseer's Bothy and the Shelter Stone are not only the dosses whose names are most likely to spring to the lips of the ordinary pedestrian, but also the ones he is most likely to have keeked into. This fact is a specific aspect of the growing blight of mountain pollution. The development of a vast holiday resort at Aviemore on Speyside has made this area the most over-used in all Scotland. But it is less than 25 years ago that Aviemore was a sleepy village, and this 'north-west frontier' of the Cairngorms regarded as the ultimate in remoteness by parties who approached, not by Aviemore, but by Braemar, for the long weekend that any trip further than Luibeg required. Now, while the Shelter stone is still 15 plus miles from Braemar, a climber who has walked there can meet the day trippers who descend from Cairngorm, which they have ascended in minutes by ski-lift. *O tempora, o mores!*

Corrour Bothy is probably the most famous bothy in the world, and it is probably also the oldest still in use. But it was not the first. Such distinction seems to belong to the bothies in Glen Einich, over the Cairn Toul/Braeriach massif, known as 'John of Corrour's Bothies'. Sadly, these were demolished, though the floor of the upper bothy remains visible. They were always open, and their endower stipulated that there should always be a bag of oatmeal in them for the benighted traveller. Though still in use in the 1930s, these bothies had passed into oblivion long before the present writer put on his boots. W.H. Murray mentions the bothy, and in *Mountaineering in Scotland*, records the timeless delight of reading his pals' names on the wall.

Corrour, on the other hand was functioning as a bothy at the turn of the century. Seton Gordon recalled that he received shelter in the bothy from John Macintosh, a deer watcher and piper, and that one night the two men were piping by the fire when a herd of deer appeared and danced on their hind legs to the music. Macintosh's predecessor, Charles Robertson, could apparently charm the mice from the walls with his pipes, and get them to perch on his boots. Others have recalled the bothy being furnished with box bed and chair long after it was abandoned. Though ruinous after World War II, it was restored in 1950, and has subsequently been maintained by the MBA since the mid 1960s.

Corrour has become a stopping off point for those 'doing' the Lairig Ghru, and is thus heavily used, as this walk has become increasingly popular. The accessibility of the bothy has also been increased by the construction of a footbridge over the Dee, where previously a wide, swift and sometimes deep crossing afforded a spice of adventure. It is unlikely that today's bothier would find solitude in Corrour.

The approach to the bothy from Luibeg, by the Allt Preas nam Maeirleach begins as a magical walk through Scots pine forests, by a sandy track, until, the country becoming wilder, the Lairig Ghru looms into sight, and the bothy is attained after entry to the lower reaches of the pass. The bothy is an excellent centre for the ascent of Cairn Toul and Braeriach, but that of Macdui is not recommended, as it takes you through the infamous boulder field and involves a gruelling ascent. A sporting short scramble is the ascent of Devils Peak (originally another part of Old Nick's anatomy, rendered harmless *anglice*), via the gulley which splits the boiler-plate slabs, and direct access to which is gained from Corrour.

The bothy itself is solid, though small (only one room) and spartan. In bygone days it may have been furnished and floored, but now bare stone walls and bare earth are its portion. The only concession to luxury was a table, and what a table! Made out of concrete, its artisan had been deficient in skill, and it sported a huge indentation. Into this poured paraffin, wax, tea, food, soup and other matters indescribable, and hard to remove. It was generally held that the benighted traveller need not starve in Corrour: he could make soup from the nourishing stock encrusted in the table's recess. There was a fireplace at Corrour, but many with little acumen stood around looking wistfully at it, as if waiting for the next coal delivery to pass by. But Glen Geusachan is the Glen of the Pines, and all around Corrour are the roots of the ancient Caledonian Forest, soaked in resin and embedded in the peat hags. They burn for hours, giving out their unique glow and smell. Though bog pines are difficult to light, heather roots make excellent kindling to get the pines started. A good blaze can compensate for the lack of seating accommomodation and the cold, rough, damp floor. (Since this was written, Corrour has apparently been upgraded somewhat.)

A party of mountaineers was occupying Corrour, on a miserable night of blizzards and wind. In the fireplace the pine logs crackled. Suddenly the door burst open and in stormed a party of soldiers. The occupants' first feeling was that a military coup had taken place, and all known malcontents were to be wiped out. However what transpired revealed that 'come the revolution' the malcontents may stand a better chance than anticipated. The guests turned out to be merely military apprentices out on a 'survival' exercise in the Cairngorm winter, doubtless in preparation for an invasion of Siberia. But deciding that camping in a Cairngorm blizzard was too much, with tents collapsing around them, they decided to strike camp and seek the comfort of the bothy. They had abandoned their gear, except sleeping bags, and forded the river in the dark, unaware of the whereabouts of the bridge. Amazingly, none were killed. The assembled company of anarcho-unilaterists felt deeply pleased that in mountain craft they were clearly a match for the military puppies, who stood around wet and sheepish.

'Fit'll you lads dae fan the Russians come?' quipped one mountaineer. However, the feeling that in hand-to-hand combat they were probably at a disadvantage compared with their enforced guests restrained further banter. The military began to arrange themselves, furthest from the fire, and a cramped night was spent with only oblique references to anti-militarist outrages. In recent years the Army has been prone to increase its use of bothies for training purposes, doing nothing to maintain them. One one occasion a bothier arrived at a Galloway bothy to find it sandbagged, and a military exercise going on! The military are also, without exception, the filthiest users of bothies, and leave rubbish scattered profusely.

As an alternative to Armageddon, little can compare with the Feshie, surely the most beautiful stretch of river in the Cairngorms. Wide, and with sandy banks, its sides are girt with pines and scented juniper bushes that grow thick and high alongside it. Little wonder that this area was a favourite haunt of the Victorian landscape and animal painter Landseer, now very much in fashion again, after decades of obscurity. Though known as Landseer's Bothy, the hut of Ruigh-aiteachain is not in fact where the painter stayed. Next to the bothy a chimney stack rises, like a monument. This is all that remains of the building used by the famous painter. Above the fireplace there remained for many years, as the building deteriorated, the fabled frescoes of the stags painted by the artist. Gavin mentions the bothy as intact, and the frescoes in good condition in 1929, and reproduced drawings of them. Seton Gordon indicates that they were still there in 1947, and claims their shelter was a chapel, and Firsoff, who lived at the head of Glen Feshie, mentions them as extant in the early 1960s. Now the frescoes, like the building, have vanished.

Landseer's is, if anything, more used than Corrour. A recent examination of the hut-book showed that fewer than a handful of days in the last six months had seen it empty. But the company met on a certain occasion was not quite what was expected. The wood surrounding Landseer's is used as sheltered grazing for a herd of white horses, who compete for the lush vegetation with deer. But those horses had discovered that humans represented food, not in person, but on their persons. Weary feet were trudging towards the bothy when the first of the breed appeared, ambling towards the walkers.

Then came another. Sacks were dug into and a couple of carrots produced. The sudden drumming of hooves told that this was a mistake. The party was soon surrounded by a dozen or so mean and hungry horses, whose sturdy bulk jostled the walkers in their attempt to convey the message.

Caught in a milling herd of mustangs, and being trampled to death, didn't seem to be a good idea. The party thus engaged in as brisk a trot as heavy sacks would allow, towards the bothy. But the beasts were obviously used to such tactics, and galloped off to take up position in front of the bothy, which now seemed very far away. Skill was clearly called for; the last carrot was scattered in fragments, causing a breach in the equine defenses as they scattered to retrieve them. A rush through the breach attained the door, and imagined safety. On turning to check, there stood a real life version of the famous whisky advert. Half inside the bothy, blocking the entrance, stood the white horse you could take anywhere, and looking set to enter and wreak untold havoc. A thrust with the door managed to persuade it to retreat, but the herd remained in siege for some time. Later arrivals told similar tales of those herds of highway robbers.

Landseer's is a cosy doss. It consists of two good rooms, with a sleeping loft above the best one, and the loft gets heated by the fire. Furniture is in abundance, carved out of tree trunks, like daft garden gnome furniture. But the greatest advantage of the bothy is the fire, from limitless supplies of fallen pine or fragrant juniper bush, within strolling distance. Yet some, possibly through ignorance rather than malice, still cut live timber to burn; timber that burns very badly, since it is too 'green'.

One night in Landseer's, when the party was getting well plastered on the wine of the country, toasting socks at the fire after a day's neat navigation in a white-out on Carn Ban More, where wee Davy discovered that without gear you die, Big Davy poo-pooed the idea that this was a fire to be proud of. And he told us that in his younger days, there had been a real fire at Landseer's on a winter's night, with self-feeding logs up the lum, and the party retreating ever further back to avoid roasting, till they were pinned against the further wall, and the stone lintel above the fireplace cracked. 'Aye, and we got on oor dark glasses, stripped tae the underpants, and got a good tan.' The disbelief exhibited by the shavers present indicated a decline in respect for the older generation.

The bothy fire performs a role similar to that it performed, one supposes, in the Neanderthal caves. It is the focus of the long winter's night, lovingly and incessantly tended lest it go out. The collection of fuel is a major part of the day's work, often done after a gruelling time on the hill. It is vital as a source of warmth in freezing climes, and to ease aching limbs after freezing climbs. It is a stand-by for cooking brew-ups, a focus for conversation on its structure, the respective combustability of woods, merits of the lum's drawing power compared to others. It induces a nirvana-like stupor, especially if a dram is to hand. It is a minute link with nature, and a rupture with the commodity economy. Without the fire, a winter's night in a doss can be a misery.

Mention of the fire leads to a cautionary tale, replete with moral lessons.

They could only have been Glaswegians. The pair of them entered the bothy late in the afternoon, as the fire was already blazing. Within an hour, they were drunk. Along the five-mile road they had carried a dozen cans of beer and a bottle of whisky. As they voraciously waded through this lot, one of them from time to time said, 'Sorry we cannae offer youze yins any: we've no got much.'

They attacked the pile with such intensity that in less than two hours they had finished it. Then they sank into a morose silence, a little at a loss. There was an Englishman there, of the middle classes, who had come to ski and discover himself in the mountain fastness, and he was appalled at having to share the doss with drunken Glesca keelies. So appalled was he that he lapsed into a glowering silence, and poked the fire with such intensity that it threatened to go out. His annoyance was increased when he was drenched with froth from one of the offending beer cans, and no apology was offered. He retaliated by pointing out the imminent demise of the fire, and stating that his contribution to wood collecting was over.

This galvanised the keelies into action. One was a wee fly man, the other a big lump, who appeared to be a daftie. One could have searched far for nearer duplicates of George and Lennie in *Of Mice And Men*. 'We'll get wood, we'll get wood', ejaculated the fly man, to mollify the company. 'Shuggie, go and get wood.'

And off Shuggie dutifully went, to perform his labours. His lumbering frame seemed capable of immense feats of lumberjacking. In a few minutes he returned, looking a bit puzzled, and holding in his hands a pile of twigs any self-respecting crow would have deemed insufficient for a nest. These he deposited on the fire, and the fly man clearly regarded their contribution to the common weal as completed. He then rocked himself into a semi-stupor by the fire, which other hands obtained the means to replenish.

Booze they had brought, but their catalogue of ommissions was vast. They had no tin opener. The Englishman glowered. They had no cups, and used empty food tins. They'd forgotten their torch, had no candles, and, appallingly, no tea. As a brew-up started, the fly man asked: 'Any chance of some tea bags, pal?'

'Sorry, we cannae offer youze any, we've no much,' came the reply.

Fly man winced at hearing his own words quoted, and he and Shuggie stumbed off into the night. In their absence the Englishman raved and ranted about drunkards spoiling the hills, and so forth. Now, while the keelies had gone a bit over the score, this was equally so; some give and take is necessary in such culture clashes. The taciturn and to them 'wet' Englishman was like a red rag to a bull, and the Glaswegians, sensing uncannily that they were not welcome, over -acted accordingly. They came back, armed, if not with a pipe of peace, at least with a more respectable offering of wood than before. As they deposited it, they were informed: 'There's tea in the dixies if you want it.'

This and the walk sobered them up, and sensing an opening, the fly man said: 'Where's the crack, then? This is no' a cheery party.'

Exchanges of information followed, a sparring and sussing out took place. The fly man turned out to be experienced and knowledgeable, but constantly over-reached himself, and made errors, that were quietly corrected by Shuggie, who pointed out his misplacement of bothies and misquotations from famous authors. 'Aye, that's right, Shuggie, that's what I meant,' was the reply. Shuggie wasn't daft after all, and here was a symbiosis at first unsuspected.

The Englishman's ears began to prick up, and though continuing his errant vestal virgin role (he didn't understand a fire needs a heart), he began to realise that the keelies had something to offer after all. More tea was brewed, grub and gossip passed round, and the evening ended on a note of high spirits.

In the morning, as all prepared to decamp, the keelies remained abed, and looked set to do so for some time. The Englishman bade them goodbye. 'Maybe see you again sometime,' said the fly man. And the parties went their separate ways.

Of the Etchachan Hut, what can be said? A dreadful doss in a marvellous location. Behind it lies one of the finest Cairngorm crags, with routes like Djibangi etched on it as clearly as in the guide books. Behind that again lie the waters of Loch Etchachan, at 3700 feet the highest in Britain, and the heart of the Cairngorms. But the doss! Built 30 years ago, it is a concrete monstrosity, with a corrugated iron roof, and vandal proof. But it drips condensation in all weathers, and when full, huge drops fall and stream down the walls. The floor is earth and constantly wet. There is nowhere to sit, and no fire, though there was in the beginning. Unless at the height of summer, it is a place to go with a definite object, i.e., climbing, in mind, rather than to enjoy a weekend of cameraderie. Even the hut book is damp and seems ready to fall to pieces in your hands. A combination of these things makes Etchachan one of the coldest bothies imaginable. Such was the prevalent misery there that all memories have been anaesthetised. Rather than dwelling on it, we pass on, as the traveller should, to the fairly near, and much more romantic, Shelter Stone.

Gladstone, when at Balmoral, did a 40 mile round walk to see it, and the Cairngorm Club, older by a whisker than the S.M.C, was founded underneath it. Its weight has been computed, its praises sung, and, alas, its environs littered.

If Corrour is the most famous bothy, the Shelter Stone must be the most famous howff in Scotland. Lying like an intrusion in the hoof of the gigantic Loch Avon horseshoe, it was formed when glacial action deposited a pile of boulders near the head of the Loch. The Stone is probably the oldest inhabited spot in the area, and was said to have been the lair of a band of outlaws at one time, but it is only one of several natural shelters in the region. But the Shelter Stone is the biggest and best of the lot, more like a cave than a howff, it is big enough to stand in, and a party of several can sleep and cook in it with comfort. At least one trip to the Shelter Stone has become an essential task for all hill-men,. Seton Gordon, no bothier, visited it, and spent a night there, and even some of the Glasgow climbers of the 1930's braved the walk to it, though it can't be seen from the road, and spent an epic time there. Humble investigated the Shelter Stone's Visitors' Books and found that from 1924 to 1954, a total of 13,147 people had dossed there, an average of over one a night. But now the day tripper who can drop down from the top of Cairngorm, and pollute the place in more ways than one, has destroyed much of the romance of the Stone. In the 1960s it was an ambitious expedition, requiring the establishment of a base camp at Luibeg on Friday night. Then it was a hard walk into Loch Avon the next day, leaving the Sunday of a long weekend for the hill, and the next day for the epic walk back to Braemar.

The howff is roomy, but it is damp, and in most weathers very cold, with only the heat provided by the stoves. Those contemplating over-nighting there would be well advised to be prepared for physical hardships, in an area that seems to collect the worst of the Cairngorm weather.

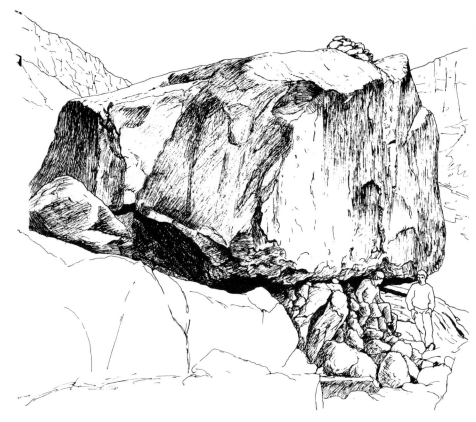

The Shelter Stone

In the past, only the last of the brave, those tempered by earlier trips to more luxurious dosses, made the trip to the Shelter Stone. To justify such a trip, a reason was necessary, and that reason could only be to climb. Or, at least, that was the theory. This aim increased the problems, since added to ordinary gear, ropes and ironmongery had to be carried. Generally, it transpired that there were compelling reasons for breach, rather than observance, of the aim.

Crawling from the Shelter Stone, the novice experiences a feeling of vertigo, as he stares at Carnetchachan and the Shelter Stone Crag. Fearsome is the only word to describe it, and for a long time it was designated 'unclimbable'. The weak-kneed may still feel this was a wise designation. One weekend the Stone was occupied by a trio who had gone through all the agony of getting there, in order to climb. As one of them emerged in the early morning to relieve nature, his eyes lit on an awesome sight. There, as if about to leap, stood the dreaded object. There comes a moment of self-discovery in every mountaineer's life, when he realises his limitations. And this was his moment.

No way was he scrambling over that death-dealing wall! His future was now clear: gentleman mountaineer in the Seton Gordon tradition, a pundit of the peaks, not a conquistador of the crags. But then there was the question of losing face.....

The weather came to his rescue. As his companions, Stumpy and Desperate Dan, emerged from their subterranean sleeping place, a greasy rain began to fall. The companions fumed and cursed at the weather which made climbing impossible (granite is treacherous when wet), which allowed their partner to argue boldly for a direct attack on one of the climbs. Beaten back, his next suggestion, to reconnoitre some of the main climbs on the face, in preparation for the next visit, was accepted. The day was spent in planning future exploits, whose avoidance would take some doing.

But his pals' blood was up, and a return visit quickly planned. Preceded by a long stretch of unbroken good weather, the dreaded weekend loomed. They waited for him at the Guild St. Bus station, and he arrived, to consternation, in company.

'Fit did ye bring him for? Ye cannae climb wi a dog!' cried Dan.

He replied, in what he hoped was a convincing way, that no one could be found to take care of the animal. Pinnacle Gully was the limit of his scrambling that weekend, accompanied by the offically cursed, but really never so welcome, best friend. It took his companions a little longer, and a series of epics, bivouacing in whiteouts, and benighted on crags in the dark, before they too, discovered their limitations, and abandoned aspirations to appear in the Pantheon of all-time greats. Like Gilgamesh, most of us have to swop the desire for immortality for the delights of companionship and the fireside, which are 'also the lot of man.'

From Corrour, the Lairig Ghru snakes northwards to the Pools of Dee, and thence drops to Speyside. There are possibly more custom-built huts in that part of the Cairngorms than anywhere in Scotland. These obviously lack a certain amount of the charm associated with howffs and bothies, and no-one could call the Sinclair Hut romantic, for example. Perched like a pill box on a shoulder high above the Lairig path, it is severely functional. Why it was built there seems a mystery, since it requires a long descent to the pass for water, and on the return, most of the precious liquid is guaranteed to be spilt. It is a cold, fireless doss, but at least wooden benches enable you to sleep off the concrete floor. The main beauty of the place is the view back up the forbidding Lairig pass, and that down towards gentle Speyside. This descent takes you through the lovely Rothiemurchus forest, probably the largest area of Scots pine still intact, haunt of the red squirrel and capercaillie, which seems to demolish branches as it flies crashing through the forest.

After an arduous day, ascending Macdui, descending to the pools of Dee, and then ascending Braeriach, a weary mountaineer was making his way towards the Sinclair hut, anticipating a cheerless night ahead. On staggering up to the hut, the contents of his dixies more over his breeches than in the pan, a light was noticed within. Reinvigorated, and anticipating an evening of pleasant crack, he crossed the threshold. An old man sat within, as if in a trance. He did not discover the name of this Gerontius, but he kept going on about Arthur. Arthur apparently kept him from the summits now, and confined him to the valleys, as well as disturbing his sleep. Perhaps Arthur was the brother-in-law, with whom he 'didn't get on', thus spending two-thirds of the year wandering from bothy to bothy, only emerging to collect his disability pension. That was it, his mysterious companion was Arthur Itis! Spurning medical advice that he should rest, this old man of the hills found that on the contrary, constant exercise materially improved his condition. No longer able to scale the heights, glen walks were his speciality, and he regularly passed from Fort William to Dalwhinnie, and from Aviemore to Blair Atholl. The latter was his destination this time, and it was from the old man that the listener first heard of the fabled Tarf Hotel, where he was headed, and of Shenagag in the shadow of Beinn a Ghlo. He had been everywhere, from Sandwood Bay, when the Bothy was still by the shore, in the most lovely location in the world, to fabled Sheneval. He knew the Geldie in its days of glory, and Landseer's when the frescoes were still to be seen.

As the evening waned, he talked of bothies in the west with baths and hot water systems that could still be worked, and of winter nights in railway huts on Rannoch moor. All the Cairngorm bothies he knew, except one. Even this *Seanachaidh* didn't know the location of the secret doss on Beinn a Bhuird, and his listener felt it no crime to tell him, despite the old man's feigned indifference. His gear was old, his sleeping bag thin, boots much patched and his provisions not of the most substantial. As he shared in the meal of the younger man, the latter was reminded of Scott's lines in the *Lay of the Last Minstrel*:

The way was long, the wind was cold,
The Ministrel was infirm and old,
his withered cheek and tresses gray
Seem'd to have known a better day.

Here indeed was the archetypical figure, the last wandering bothier, an Odysseus of the mountains. Scornful of the MBA ('Holiday homes, that's their aim!'), and a desperate individualist, he had carved himself a satisfying corner in the cosmos. After a while he retreated into a non-communicative silence, and half-shut his rheumy eyes. But those of his companion had been opened, and his limited horizons breached. The Cairngorms, where previously he had felt all bothies lay, now seemed quite small. Out there lay Sheneval, Sourlies and other dosses, beneath mountains with names as romantic. A determination to widen horizons was made. As the old man headed south for the Tarf, the younger headed north, mind fertile with projects new. Cairngorm bothies might have become over-run, but out there were other wildernesses of promise.

GLENCOE

Ben 'An, the Whangie, that is where they started. Safe places, short climbs, good belays. Excitement and adventure within easy reach of Glasgow. But the appetites thus created were sharpened by news of other, greater places. Glencoe and the Buachaille Etive Mhor. Big climbs, hard, a place in which reputations were made. They would have to go there. In the '50s and '60s the first journeys would have been achieved in many different ways. Some would have gone with friends on the back of their motorbikes, others would have hitch-hiked, but others would have gone by bus — club buses, the Rannoch, the Langside — they helped the young Glaswegians make that first important journey. The Langside supplied tents and if they took them, they would arrive and camp at Coupel Bridge in a darkness that hid the delights to come. In the morning they would see it. The Buachaille Etive Mhor bursts out of the western-most reaches of Rannoch Moor, and the sight of it takes the breath away from newcomers. Their short experience in the gentler places did not prepare them for this. It is massive. The morning sunlight slants across its eastern aspects and reveals a series of buttresses piled on top of one another to form the perfect triangular shape that every mountain should have. It was something they would never forget. The start of something in their lives, something that would remain no matter what other mountains they visited: a place they would come back to and enjoy again and again.

For the regulars in the '50s and '60s, Glencoe was not, strictly speaking, bothy country, but there were a number of huts and barns where climbers could lay their heads. However, our concern is firmly focussed on the top (east) end of the glen, for in those days the Glasgow lads would never have thought about staying lower down. Perhaps those individuals, who saw themselves as being a bit tougher than your average climber, saw a reflection of themselves in the harsher geography and climate at the top of the glen. Not for them the warmer climes of the Clachaig and village area. That was where the occasional visitor stayed, and a lot of them were *English!* More likely than such base prejudices, the choice of accommodation had something to do with the location of the climbs, for although the West Face of Aonach Dubh and the slabs of Glen Etive were being developed around that time, the Buachaille was still regarded by many as the main hill

For those who were not attached to any mountaineering club, Cameron's barn at Altnafeadh was the only choice. From the '30s to the late '60s the structure that housed the ragged fraternity of the hills was the concrete box that stands on the right hand side of the road going west. Borthwick tells us that this was built by the men who laid the new road, as a replacement for a building that stood in its path. However, the tenants of Altnafeadh could not have thought much of it, for they used the older buildings across the road for their animals, giving the newer one to the climbers. Probably the reason for this was that the concrete building was extremely cold, and while it was alright for those mad climbers, no sensible crofter would winter his beasts in it. Later, when Mr Cameron retired and the house was purchased by a Belgian aristocrat, various informal groups and clubs moved into different parts of the old, warmer buildings. The Langside had a large part to themselves. The Etive, a newer club which had split from the Langside and was composed of wild, anarchistic fellows, had another. There was even a 'Ladies' Doss'. Nowadays, the barn does not appear to be used by climbers, so it cannot be recommended as an open doss.

In the 1930s, Borthwick in his book *Always a Little Further*, made the point that Mackay's Barn, as it was then called, provided shelter not only for climbers but also for tramps and other 'gentlemen' of the road. By the 1960s the welfare state had removed the need for most of those characters to roam the highways and byways of Scotland, and it was almost exclusively used by climbers. Not that this meant the clientele was any less exotic than before.

Thus, for many a sixteen year old it was in Cameron's Barn that real education began. The lessons to be learned were not the kind obtainable in schools and universities, and the most important was that the world was full of people who were different from those previously experienced. Here the middle class student met the shipyard worker, the conservative the radical and the timid the bold. Ideas were exchanged, books were recommended, stories were told of more adventures in distant places. Places with names like magic — the Dolomites, Chamonix, Zermatt — created a fever of ambition in the minds of wee boys from Maryhill. Horizons thus extended create a discontent with one's lot. Some gave up their jobs and devoted themselves to climbing and travelling in Europe, the Americas and Asia. Some even got jobs with the British Antarctic Survey and spent two years exploring the mountains there with dogs and sled. Many others who had failed in the school system met those who were successful, and, attracted by the student life, gained the confidence to try again. As a result lads from places like darkest Possil who had been labelled educational no-hopers found themselves at university and doing well.

It would be a mistake, however, to assume that this was a one-way process. The transplantation of middle class culture to the working class was more than balanced by the fact that most of the memorable characters were guys from the shipyards and factories of Clydeside. They had been raised on the strong oral tradition of that region, where a man's status is judged not by his income, but by his ability to tell jokes and stories and provide spontaneous fun, often at the expense of the management. Indeed, after hearing stories of life in a Glasgow shipyard, the listener could be excused for thinking that class warfare on the Clyde was carried out, not by strikes and violence, but by humour.

Tam and his crowd were a perfect example of this phenomenon. They were a loosely-knit group of Glaswegians who claimed to be communists but behaved like anarchists. They were always singing the *Red Flag* or the one about *Defending the U.S.S.R.*. They were great talkers and although their topics were by no means limited to politics, many a politically naive youngster first heard about the iniquities of capitalism and the class struggle during the late night debates that took place by the light of guttering candles in the stalls of the barn.

No-one in that freewheeling group, least of all Tam, would admit to having or being leaders. But as Tam was certainly the most visible and the most audible, he tends to linger in the mind as the most memorable. His appearance was that of a small man whose girth, enlarged by a fear of dehydration, did nothing to discourage that impression. Above his rounded frame was a chubby face strangely elongated by a hair line that had retreated from some early onslaught of the ageing process. This was the El Alamein of Tam's hairline. Here the hair had dug in to resist time, and although it did not have the means to fight back to the Tobruk of his forehead, there was to be no further break through on this front for many years to come. Tam also had bad eyesight, and so the most striking feature of his face was the heavy-framed glasses that carried the thick lenses he required. Under those milk bottle bottoms, Tam's eyes bulged with excitement as he stood at a bar, pint in one hand, cigarette in the other, telling some story or expounding some theory of society.

The philosophy that lay behind Tam's line of argument was often complex and sometimes contradictory, for Tam, like many of his fellow Clydesiders, managed to embrace in himself a number of countervailing ideologies popular in that area. It is not unusual to find men who are members of both the Communist Party and the Orange Order, who are shop stewards and moneylenders and bookies' runners, all at the same time. In Tam's case it was a mixture of Communism and Orangeism, and while the former dominated his thoughts in his youth, in his middle age he showed more interest in the Orange banner than the Red Flag.

Stories about the exploits of Tam and his crowd are legion, but perhaps the most amusing is the 'Great Bus Conductress Pie Assault Caper'. The lads were on a service bus that was heading up north one Friday night. They had been in the pub and were probably a wee bit noisy, singing songs and telling jokes. The conductress came up the bus to remonstrate with them, and being a formidable lady of that now extinct breed, she soon had a bit of order. Unfortunately, that did not last long, because flying through the air came a pie. As it was of the Scottish mutton variety, softish with a hard crust round the edge, when it hit the conductress in the face it not only hurt it also made a mess. The conductress's reaction was immediate and furious. She attacked the grenadier of pies with such venom his pals felt that they had to defend him. In the melee that followed the driver took immediate if rather dramatic action. He drove the bus to the nearest police station, where they were all arrested and put in the cell until they could appear before the Sheriff. When they duly appeared in his court, the Sheriff took a dim view of their behaviour, and asked the guilty party why he threw the pie at the conductress. Creative to the end, the reply came, 'Well, I didn't mean to hit her. I was passing the pie down the bus and she just got in the road.' But creativity and imagination were not enough, for Tam was fined enough to keep him out of the pubs and off the mountains for a good few weeks.

Willie of the Langside was another colourful character who appeared at Cameron's around that time. The fascination he exercised over the other inmates was not due to his climbing or outdoor skills, but, strangely enough, to his abilities in a world largely unknown to men who spent their spare time in the hills. Willie was an early swinger, whose sophisticated knowledge of city life was a source of wonderment and some slight envy to those who heard his tales of Glasgow pubs and dance halls. He awoke in them the vague feeling that their devotion to climbing might be excluding them from another, perhaps better, world. Secluded dinners in fancy restaurants with exciting and perfumed women. Expensive clothes and dancing the night away in the 'Loc', the 'Magic Stick' and the 'Flaming O'.

Willie's delight in city life meant that his approach to climbing was unique. He was ahead of his time, and was wired for sound long before today's personal stereos became fashionable. He was very keen on the Beatles and the Stones, and he used to strap a portable tape recorder on his back so he could enjoy the music as he climbed. Unfortunately, the recorders of those days were not equipped with headphones, so everyone in hearing distance was also treated to Willie's choice of music. Needless to say, many traditionalists did not approve of Willie, tapes blasting out 'Twist and Shout', dancing about on some ledge halfway up the Rannoch Wall.

Others contributed to the lively weekend life of the barn and although the hilarity created by such people as Tam and Willie added immense enjoyment and interest to the experience, most were there for the climbing. Even Tam, not the world's fittest man, went up the hill for that purpose. So even though Cameron's, with its cold concrete floor, was a most uncomfortable place to stay, it provided a grand base for climbing in Glencoe, for it gave easy access to the Buachaille's wonderful selection of summer and winter climbs.

Among its easier climbs, the North Face Route, Agag's Groove and January Jigsaw must rate among the finest 'V. Diff's' in Britain. The last named two are found on the Rannoch Wall, and are particularly good climbs, with exhilarating situations on steep rock. The final pitch of January Jigsaw can be difficult to follow, and often the idlers on the ridge below are questioned by some worried leader who has lost his way. Some individualistic people scorn such tactics and boldly strike out where their instincts take them. One guy turned left instead of right at the bottom of Satan's Slit, climbed a horrible greasy groove, and then, much to his second's horror, traversed horizontally without runners for over 100 feet to the top of Agag's Groove.

Another fine climb, Red Slab, is a good example of the multitude of horrors that lurk for the unwary in the Scottish grading system. Graded 'Severe' in the old, red-bound S.M.C. guide of 1959, its second pitch often caught out the moderate climber who expected to get good protection.   This pitch is long and its crux is on small holds on steep exposed rock.   Often the leader's nerve is weakened by the sight of good holds on a bulge to the right, and onlookers have sometimes been horrified to see people scrambling up this in a most undignified fashion.

Obviously there are also good, harder climbs.   Crows's Nest Crack and Hangsman's Crack give a nice combination on the East Face of the North Buttress, while Bludger's, the Link and Revelation do the same on the West Face.   Then, for the real tigers, Gallows Route, Shibboleth and Carnivore offer excellent tests for their skills.

In the winter the Buachaille is an exciting mountain on which the enthusiast will find plenty to interest and test.   Crowberry Gully, Gully Buttress and North Buttress are all extremely good climbs for the competent who do not want to tackle the hardest of climbs. Sometimes the winter provides bizarre experiences.

It was one of those days that climbers dream about.   The sky was clear of cloud, the air crisp and moor and hill were clad in firm ice and snow.   The lads, the artist and the teacher, had gone up the hill from Jacksonville with some friends to do Crowberry Gully.   Their minds were changed on reaching the steep shelf that lies beneath the East Face of North Buttress.   Here they decided that it was too good a day to spend in a gully they had done before.   North Buttress, in contrast, looked especially inviting.   A cocktail of delights: pillars of reddish rock, laced with beautiful green ice, all lit up by the morning sun.   They had not done this in winter and, even though they would miss a good pitch of the direct route by traversing in at this level, they decided to have a go.

It all started well enough.   The artist led up some steep runnels of ice that led diagonally up the side of the Buttress.   The ice was perfect.   Crampons and ice axes bit firmly into it, giving the climber the peace of mind that leads to perfect stability and quick progress. Soon the artist stood on a large ledge above which there was a chimney whose right side overhung slightly. There he belayed and brought up his companion.

The teacher eyed the chimney with suspicion. Steep and rather bare of ice, it looked horrible. Moreover, the exit at the top, capped as it was by a large boulder, promised difficulties. Nevertheless, duty must be done, and he must prove himself in this field of manly endeavour. Muttering to himself about the unfairness of things, he edged, with some apprehension, towards the rock.

It was awkward. The slight overhang threw him out of balance, and his crampons were more on rock than they were on ice. The front points pivoted on the small holds, adding to his feelings of insecurity. He managed to struggle up to a point where the chimney widened underneath the capstone. There he could rest, and decide at his leisure which side of the boulder to use for an exit.

On the right, the start looked easy enough, but the higher his eye went the more difficult it looked. In contrast, on the left the start looked hard. Thin ice on steepish rock. However a couple of moves on this would bring him on to easy ground that led to a belay ledge. He decided to go leftwards.

Swinging his axe and hammer into good hard snow high up, he stepped out, placing his front points as delicately as he could on the thin, steep ice. There was the sound of skittering ice, metal on rock, and there he was hanging by his hands on the wooden shafts of his ice tools, while his feet swung helplessly in mid-air.

His memory of what happened after that is a bit of a blur. Fear, of course, lurched through his body, and he could hear his heart beating alarmingly loud. Sheer lust for survival then took over. Without thinking for a moment that they would not hold, he pulled mightily on his ice axe and hammer, and scrambled on to the ledge. Once he had got his breath back, he turned to shout down to the artist something daft and reassuring like: 'Christ, that was desperate!' But no words came. Just some unintelligible noises spluttered forth, as if he were chewing a mouthful of toffee.

'Um hum un hun goum.' What's this, he thought, have I lost the power of speech? He tried again. 'Um hum on humplithum.' Then he realised what had happened. It was his false teeth, broken by a mighty clenching of the jaw at the point of maximum effort, that were preventing him from making an intelligent communication.

After that, the climb went without incident. Up a nice steep pitch of green ice, then up a smaller pitch before the angle eased back, announcing the summit ridge. On top, they met their friends who had made good time in Crowberry. Out came the cameras to record the magnificent day. In the traditional summit picture, one man is not smiling.

For the men who put up the special routes there must be a special place to stay. Such a place is found about a mile and half south-east of Altnafeadh on the south bank of the river. This is Jacksonville, a low black hut which is the home of the famous, or some might say infamous, Creagh Dhu Mountaineering Club. When the C.D.M.C. first started to use the site where the present structure stands the accommodation was very primitive, merely an old tarpaulin flung over the corner of a disused sheep fank. That did not prevent that generation of the Creagh Dhu making their extremely important contribution to post-war climbing in Scotland. Prior to June 1946, when Cunningham and McGonigle put up Crows's Nest Crack and Shattered Crack, there were only four recorded climbs of V.S. standard on the Buachaille, and three of those were gullies. By August 1958, when Cunningham and Moon snatched Carnivore from Willans, various members of the C.D.M.C. had added 26 new routes of that standard.

The present hut was built in the summer of 1960, and got its rather transatlantic sounding name from a guy named Jackson who was a leading light during the building. When finished, the walls consisted of a single layer of tarpaulin suspended on a wooden frame. As time went by some improvements were made and the walls were first lined

Jacksonville

80

with wood and then by another layer of tarpaulin. Bunks were built by McLean but some members did not seem to appreciate them, and they were dismantled when he went to Canada. Only the middle tier was any good. If you slept on the floor underneath it you were likely to feel claustrophobic. If you slept on the top tier your nose brushed against the ceiling. As one guy remarked, it was like being a bread roll in a baker's oven.

One improvement that has never been made is the building of a strong locked door. This is strange, because the Creagh Dhu have always insisted that the hut is for club members and friends only. This view has become hardened in recent years due to rather careless use of the hut by people doing the West Highland Way. There seems to be a number of reasons why the club never got round to putting a lock on the door. It is the most unbureaucratic of clubs. Keys would mean arrangements, arrangements would mean appointing officers and keeping records. Such things are not in keeping with the *laissez faire* approach of most of its members.

Then, of course, there was their reputation. They were the Creagh Dhu Mountaineering Club. A famous club, full of terrible hard men who would eat any interloping 'greenhorn' for breakfast. It is probably their ignorance of this that has emboldened the West Highland Wayers to enter such a hallowed place.

Finally, if the Club's reputation could not stop unwelcome guests, there was always the river. The river figured largely in the consciousness of the members. It was a kind of virility symbol, for whereas other groups merely walked a few yards from their transport to pitch their tents or go to Cameron's or Lagangarbh (the S.M.C. hut), the regulars at Jacksonville had to take off at least their boots and socks, and plunge into the icy cold water. Still, the numbing cold prevented them from feeling the pain inflicted by the sharp shingle. In the winter it was much worse. Heavy rain could turn the river into a raging cataract that had to be treated with extreme care. Often there was snow on the bank, and visitors had to run through it, barefooted, to the hut. Inside, they would join the others flogging their feet and rolling about in agony as life began to return to them. Sometimes the river was covered with a thin layer of ice and people would arrive in the hut and wonder why there was blood on the floor. It came, of course, from their bare ankles, cut as they broke through the ice. The interesting thing is that very few in those days ever organised themselves to bring sandshoes or wellingtons To do so would have invited suspicions about their masculinity.

The river could also be a source of embarassment. In inclement weather when the water level was high, it was standard practice to take off one's trousers and put them in a polythene bag. In this way, people could get across the river and down to the pub at Kingshouse so as to enjoy the evening in comfort. If it was still raining at closing time, then off came the trousers for the walk back. One foul night Willie and Alastair were following this traditional form of behaviour when, as they arrived at the Etive road end, the weather suddenly cleared up and the rain stopped. 'Great,' thought the lads, 'We'll get the trousers back on.' After all, it is not very dignified being caught in the lights of a passing car clad in a bunnet, an oil skin jacket and big boots, but no trousers.

At that time there was a telephone box at the road end, and some deep puritanical impulse in the two lads made them go inside it in order to adjust their dress. It was then that the police arrived. At first they suspected vandalism, but when they opened the door of the kiosk it was obvious from the look they exchanged that they thought they had caught two lads at an activity illegal then, even in private. The two constables kept their cool and went into the time-honoured routine of their calling.

'What's your name, son?' The question was directed at Willie, who had managed to get his trousers on.

'Willie.......' came the reply.

The constable then nodded at Alistair, a damp wretch whose knees were still exposed to the probing light of the police torch. 'And yours?'

'Alistair.....'

There was a long silence as the officers grappled with the immensity of the supposed crime they had discovered. Then as if to get quickly to the heart of the matter, one of them asked in his lilting Highland accent, 'And where iss Alistair's trousers?'

The two lads managed to convince the policemen of their innocence of any wrong-doing, but Alistair made the mistake of telling the story to his friends, who, with wicked glee began to use it as a greeting. Thus, everytime Alistair appeared on the hill, the gullies and buttresses rang with cries of 'And where iss Alistair's trousers?' Alistair, of course, was not amused, but everyone else thought it quite hilarious.

Crossing the river perhaps four times a day fits in well with the view of some authorities on the essential nature of mountaineering. Climbing, according to this Outward Bound type philosphy, is all about building the character. Subject young lads to difficulty and danger, make them miserable and wet and you give them back-bone and moral fibre or some such thing. There is no doubt that the members of the Creagh Dhu, working class though they were in the main, were brim full of those peculiarly middle class qualities. However, most of them would never have gained undying admiration for their sober-minded approach to life. They were men of broad interests and habits, characteristics which were reflected in the amount of time and effort spent at Jacksonville on pursuits that would bring a quiver to the stiff upper lips of Ullswater and Eskdale.

Along with most other climbers, the members of the Creagh Dhu indulged in trials and exhibitions of strength. People were always doing one-armed pull-ups in the rafters of Jacksonville, or challenging each other to arm wrestling contests. Not much there that runs counter to the Outward Bound philosophy, you might think. Yet it was the extreme nature of some of those trials of strength that on reflection seems most bizarre. Take for example the strange tale of Wee Davy of the Creag Dhu and Big Jim of the Edinburgh S.M.C.

The two groups that those lads represented were friendly rivals in the world of climbing. Davy, a shipyard worker from Clydebank, was, and still is, immensely strong. He used to do all the most difficult boulder problems of the time in his bare feet. His magnificent stature — muscles would bulge and ripple with every movement — came about after medical advice that he should build himself up after a serious childhood illness. This he did with a vengeance by weight-training and wrestling. Indeed, so good was he at this latter activity he used to enjoy great success in competitions at varous Highland Games. Big Jim? Well, he was just naturally big and strong. A giant of a man in whose hand a fish slice took on the proportion of a teaspoon in that of any ordinary man.

Back in the sixties, people used to speculate about the relative strength of those two very different shaped giants. Some thought that Davy, with his massive chest and shoulders, must be the stronger, while others argued that Jim, with his vastly superior height, had the advantage. At first the two strong men remained aloof from such discussions. It was as if they had little to prove to those of relatively inferior build. Yet one night at Jacksonville the rivals agreed to resolve the matter by means of a short trial of strength. It was a very simple competition in which each one would have three punches at the other's stomach. Big Jim was to go first.

With his massive fist clenched tightly, he stepped up to Davy who had taken up his position, legs apart, hands on hips, his muscular chest stuck out defiantly. The first punch thudded into Davy's solar plexus, and to the astonishment of the company he took off backward to land with a crash among primus stoves and dixies. Unharmed, he disentangled himself from the pots and stoves, and stood up to face the next blow. That was rammed home, ferocious as the first. Back went Davy among the cooking utensils, only to rise again completely unconcerned. Big Jim looked a little puzzled, for his best punches appeared to have little effect. Nevertheless he applied himself diligently to the third punch, only to see Davy pick himself up once again with a nonchalance that suggested he was rising from a nap.

Now it was Davy's turn. He crashed a mighty punch into his adversary's stomach, who, in contrast to Davy's backward motion, collapsed straight down like a sack of potatoes falling from a lorry. Poleaxed and gasping for breath, the big fellow admitted that one was enough.

'Well, that's two I owe you,' replied Davy.

The onlookers closed their mouths and shook their heads in amazement.

Twenty-odd years later one asks oneself: did the sequel really happen? Or was it the product of fading memory? Some fantasy to create interest in one's dull past? No! There they are again, those two mighty men. The stuff of myth. This time they are seen through the soft twilight of a Scottish late summer evening. They are on the bridge over the burn that runs by the Kingshouse Hotel, and Jim has annoyed Davy in some way. Did he really do it? It seems so fantastic that it must be fiction. Did he really, with exquisite grace and ease, bend down and pick the big man up, one hand on his crutch and the other at the scruff of his neck, and dangle him, head first, over the parapet? Yes, he did! He was that strong.

The dancing at Ballachulish or Glencoe village was one form of interest that got the lads into all sorts of bother. Lifts could often be begged or borrowed to get down the glen. It was getting back up that could prove difficult, especially if there was a young lady to walk back home. Big Willie had an unfortunate experience whilst pursuing this particular form of dalliance. P.A's, the special rock-climbing boot favoured at the time, were for some obscure reason thought to be suitable for the dancing. In fact, they were better designed for the bastinado than for the foxtrot. They were, as one contemporary used to say, 'foot corsets'. Sharing the general belief that the climbing boots were fine for the dancing, Willie left his comfortable walking boots in the van when he went in pursuit of pleasure at the Ballachulish Village Hall. He would dance in his P.A.s. Surely they would set him apart from the ruck, and would perhaps influence some young lady in his favour. As luck would have it, Willie found a young lady who was willing to allow him to see her home to Glencoe village. In paroxyisms of delight, he rushed to the van and demanded his walking boots. The P.A.s were fine for the dancing, but not for a long midnight walk home. Later, after his adventure with the young lady, Willie went to put his walking boots on, only to discover that while one fitted, the other was miles too small. He had been handed odd boots. It is seven long miles from the village to Jacksonville, and Willie, cursing the man who had handed out his boots, tried every combination of the footwear available to him, but in the end decided to walk with one foot bare. When he reached the 'ville, the blood blisters on that foot did not deny him the satisfaction of kicking the poor unsuspecting innocent from his deep slumber.

Another pastime not associated with character building is card games. Pontoon was very popular with some of the lads, and although large sums of money were never involved, some became so obsessed that if they lost money one weekend they would pursue the victor to wherever he was going the next, so that they could get their revenge. All night sessions were quite common, and often they would involve the lads from Edinburgh, Smith, Haston and Moriarty. Even in the coldest winter's nights the participants would sit or lie, fully dressed, complete with bunnets, in their sleeping bags, peering at the cards which were illuminated by a flickering candle. They did not seem to notice or mind that the condensation from their breath was freezing on the canvas wall of the hut. In those games, Cunningham, with all the studied coolness of a river boat gambler, seemed to be master, and, although he was skillful, his victories were probably the result of one big advantage he had over the others. That was his relative affluence, gained from his years with British Antarctic Survey, which allowed him to survive any loss of luck before taking the bank and benefitting from the advantages of that role.

Even more important was 'Wee Heidies', a fiercesome two-aside ball game played on some flat ground to the east of the hut. So seriously was this game taken that even on a bright summer's day the climbing was ignored as people risked life and limb in search of goals. Sure, they meant to go up the hill, but the games started after breakfast created such intense competition the hill tended to get forgotten. It was not as if 'Wee Heidies' was safer than rock climbing, for it involved very dangerous manoevres that took peoples' heads and faces very close to the flying fists of the very determined defenders.

The 'pitch' was defined by 'goals' made of jackets about 20 yards apart. One member of the attacking team stood on his goal line and headed the ball to his partner who had taken up a position at one side about half way between the two goals. To score, the partner had to run onto the ball and head it past the two defenders.

Big John was the meanest man to play against. Tall, he was difficult to beat as he came forward to give the attacker a physical examination. The same was true when defending — the opposition had to be prepared for minor violence. And then he argued — the ball was too high, it was by the post — he usually got his way. Others, superb climbers though they might be, were not very good at this game. Unusual for working class boys from Glasgow, they seemed to have neglected football. Their approach to the ball was haphazard — throw it up, close the eyes and poke the forehead forward. Invariably, it hit the back of their heads and shot backwards. Such lack of promise ensured an early departure for the hill.

Those activities rather put off some people who were intent on climbing. Les Brown, a famous name from England, stayed in Jacksonville when he moved to Scotland, but seemed to get a bit fed up with the constant enthusiasm for 'Wee Heidies'. However, he stayed long enough to introduce people to cunning new climbing tactics. Before setting out on a climb, he would fill his anorak pocket with stones of various sizes. He would drop them into cracks and use them as running belays. This happened long before the development of special 'nuts' used for the purpose today, and the sight of 'Chocky', as they rather aptly called him, taking on his load surprised and amused a lot of people. Some members of the club who were a bit conservative and held strong ethical views were not so happy. They held that any deviation from the original way a climb was done, and which made it safer, was a form of cheating.

Another visit to Jacksonville, a very brief one this time, actually made the glossy pages of the *Sunday Times Colour Supplement Magazine*. In an interview, Chris. Bonnington used a rather unfortunate incident at Jacksonville as an illustration of the treatment he received from climbers who were jealous of his success and reputation. In fact, his complaint was based on a misinterpretation of what actually happened that day.

He turned up early one gloriously sunny Saturday morning when the 'ville was packed out. Everybody was there: McLean, Gardner, Jimmy Ellis, Cunningham, Con. Higgins, to name but a few. They were all busy cooking their breakfasts. McLean, dressed only in some underwear of dubious vintage, was sitting in the middle of this melee, annoyed because he had just dropped his fried egg on the floor. He was scraping it up and putting it on his 'Piece' when Bonnington arrived.

'Is there a Mr. McLean here?' (he pronounced the name to rhyme with *lean*), he asked.

McLean corrected the mispronunciation of his name, and acknowledged that he was the man.

'Mr. McInnes recommended you as a climbing partner for me,' continued Bonnington in his rather posh accent. McLean, already irritated by his delinquent egg, was shocked that anyone should have the temerity to suggest such a thing. He said that no way was he going to climb with this forward stranger, and that he could leave (although it was not put as politely as that).

Bravely Bonnington stood his ground and asked around the hut, but no one would take him on, and he had to leave partnerless. Now this does appear to constitute a rather unkind and peremptory dismissal of a climber in search of like souls. That, however, is not the point. Bonnington thought he was rejected because people were jealous of him when in fact, although his reputation was growing at the time, his face was unknown to those present. To them, he was simply a pushy stranger 'chancing his arm' a bit. They simply found it incredible that a stranger should walk into a hut and demand to climb with men who were, after all, among Scotland's leading climbers. Climbing is a risk activity and people tend to participate with friends they know they can rely on. As Bonnington was unknown to them, he obviously did not fall into that category at that time.

Not all the characters who went to the 'ville were famous for their exploits on the hill. Some, like 'Malky the Alky' had other claims to fame. As his name suggests, Malky was fond of a wee refreshment. However he was no worse than many others who hung round the glen in the sixties, and it is probably the case that he got his name simply because of the tempting rhyme. That, and the fact that the most striking feature of his rather doleful face was a long nose that had a tendency to be a bit red.

Neither was it just the case that Malky was famous for owning a car at a time when few regulars on the scene had such a thing. No, it was the nature of Malky's car, whose dirty brown colour was determined partly by the manufacturer's design and partly by Malky's neglect. Neglect was probably responsible for the car's mechanical defects, the most dangerous of which was an apparently total lack of suspension.

Of course, that was before M.O.T. tests, and indeed many people felt that Malky's car was an outstanding argument for the introduction of such tests, for it showed an amazing propensity for leaving the road and hitting things.

Every journey had at least one incident that reduced Malky's pasengers, brave mountaineers though they were, to gibbering idiots. Most gave little thought to death when on the hill, but in Malky's car, many felt its bony hand on their shoulders. Yet no-one was ever seriously injured in Malky's car.

Even when, inevitably, Malky smashed his car beyond repair no-one ended up in hospital. It happened one wet winter's day in Glencoe just above the farm at Achtriochtan. Malky as usual was driving too fast for a car that was practically uncontrollable, when one of the suicidal sheep that inhabit Glencoe stepped out in front of him. Now normally, because of the car's erratic behaviour, Malky would not have hesitated in mowing the poor beast down. Cars were built to last in those days, and his especially was like a tank: Malky knew the sheep would come off worse. However, only a few weeks earlier, in following out this (from the sheep's point of view) rather draconian policy, the car had required a new radiator, and Malky was not in the mood to go through that again. So, fatefully, he made a decision to swerve and avoid the sheep. Its good fortune turned out to be Malky's hard luck story. Predictably the car took to the air as it went off the embankment and somersaulted down the hill to give the lads a better view of the Glencoe river. It landed upright, but even the most mechanically naive onlooker would have known that it had gone to meet its maker in the big car park in the sky. The body was comprehensively bashed in, steam and smoke came from the engine compartment, the wheels lay at right angles to the body. Brought up on Hollywood movies in which cars that went down ravines,, mountains and such like inevitably burst into flames, all the passengers except Malky scrambled out through the windowns. Dazed, he sat, twirling the obviously defunct steering wheel round and round, muttering to himself: 'The steering's knackered.'

Glencoe is of course a magnificent place to climb and walk. Going across the Rannoch Moor the first sight of the glen can stimulate the appetite for adventure of even the most seasoned of mountaineers. Seeing it for the umpteenth time he may reflect on the hours of enjoyment and the days of struggle spent there. For the first-time visitor, here is where plans are about to become reality; where anticipation is converted into sheer excitement.

At the glen's eastern end stands the great sentinel of the Buachaille Etive Mor. Visitors will note how it changes shape as their car speeds by the Glen Etive roadend, up towards the Jacksonville carpark. Here is the best prospect of the mountain, and many will stop just to look, even though they may be heading further north.

The eye can follow the path from Jacksonville across the moor, and then steeply up the lower, heather covered slopes to the unique

Waterfall Slab, the first resting place of many an expedition. Then on again over steep, now badly eroded paths, through broken outcrops of rock to the bottom of Curved Ridge. For the hillwalker who can cope with some rock-scrambling, Curved Ridge is the best way to ascend the Buachille. For the climber it is the only way! Passing through some of the finest rock scenery on mainland Scotland, the Ridge is the main highway through the northern precipices of the mountain.

As it starts steeply the climber's mind and body will be occupied with the task of ascending the polished rock. Easy though it may be, a slip here would be serious. After a hundred feet or so the ridge suddenly flattens out; here is the place to take in the magnificence of the surroundings. The first feature to strike the consciousness is the huge steepness of Crowberry Ridge, bounded on the right by the dark defile of Crowberry Gully, and on the left by the famous and fabulous Rannnoch Wall. Further to the right, across the lower reaches of Crowberry Gully, the outline of North Buttress can be seen. Its eastern wall is formed by the East Face of North Buttress, a short but steep rampart of fine rock on which many superb climbs can be found.

The eye, however, will be drawn back to the Crowberry Ridge and the Rannoch Wall, and perhaps the sight of a rock climber high up on Agag's Groove or January Jigsaw will spur the traveller on so as to obtain a better view of this wonderful precipice. Further up the ridge another flat place will be encountered, where on a good summer's day can be found the discarded packs of the climbers who seek to scale the wall. Here an hour or so can be idled away watching their progress to the top.

Inevitably there will be a party or two on the famous Agag's Groove, which steeply traverses the right hand section of the face from left to right. Further up and to the left someone may be climbing the airy routes of Whortleberry Wall, Red Slab or Peasant's Passage. To the uninitiated, it will look sensational, because from the distance they are watching from, the holds and belay ledges will go undetected. The climbers, seemingly so relaxed, so easy in movement, appear to stand and hold on to nothing.

Before moving on to the final steep section of the ridge, some attention must be paid to the view to the east. Shimmering in the heat haze of a warm summer's day, Rannoch Moor stretches out, broken only by its myriads of lochans, to Scheihallion some thirty miles away. The flatness of the moor is a perfect counterpoint to the rugged sharpness of the mountains at the eastern end of Glencoe.

As the climber ascends the top section of the ridge, he will continue to obtain magnificent views of the wall and the climbers on it. He will have no difficulty following the route over the well-worn rock. However, approximately three hundred feet above his last resting place the delightful scrambling comes to an abrupt end. From here there is a choice of routes. An ascent can be made of what in summer is a steep grassy slope directly across the ridge. Above this, a turn to the right is made to climb through a band of rock to the summit. Alternatively, and more interestingly, most choose to traverse around the base of Crowberry Tower into a short gully. After stopping to admire the spectacular view down the gully, or perhaps to climb to the top of the Tower, the broken rocks on the left are tackled. The exit from these is on to the top of the right fork of Crowberry Gully. From there is it is but a short distance to the summit.

Even on the coldest of days the view from this airy point will stop the progress of most. To the south-east, across Glen Etive there is the group of mountains that includes Meal a Bhuiridh, the favourite of the plank-pushing fraternity. To its right there is the ridge that comprises Sron na Criese, Clach Leatha and Stob Ghabher, which provides a grand high level walk to Bridge of Orchy. To the south-west one can see the continuing ridge of the Buachaille, a fine walk in its own right. And then to the west, down into the heart of Glencoe itself, the ridges and summits of the elegant Bidean nam Bian and Stob Coire nan Lochan. All these are on the south side of the glen.

To the north of them there is the jagged, airy outline of the Anoch

Eagach, held to be the finest ridge walk on the mainland of Scotland.

In summer, the descent of the Buachaille can be made back down Curved Ridge. This is not recommended in winter. In that often unforgiving season it is better to continue along the ridge in a south-westerly direction until a large cairn is encountered. From there one turns to the west and after approximately a quarter of a mile the top of Lagangarbh Coire is reached. From there, depending on the season, a quick scree run or glissade brings one down to a path that emerges at Lagangarbh Cottage and finally Altnafeadh. In winter, be careful. Good map and compass work is essential in mist or white-out conditions. Too early a descent to the top of Lagangarbh Coire can bring one onto some very difficult ground. This has been the cause of a number of fatal accidents. In bad weather it is a good idea to work out the required compass bearings and estimated walking times in camp or bothy. Also in winter, take care in beginning the descent of the Coire. Often the head wall will consist of steep hard neve. Some, usually early in their careers, have descended the Coire a little faster than intended, for the want of a little respect and consideration. One weekend, when there was a lot of fresh snow around a fellow jumped down the head wall to land safely in soft snow. The next week he tried the same thing again, only to take off like a toboggan down the Cresta Run. After a week of thaw and frost, the snow was brick hard.

Another walk that will introduce the newcomer to the delights of Glencoe includes its highest summit, Bidean nam Bian. Leave the road using the footpath that goes through the Larig Eilde to Glen Etive. After about half a mile leave the path and cut diagonally up onto the ridge of Bhienn Fhada. From here an excellent high level walk can be enjoyed round to the summit of Bidean. After enjoying the wonderful views of mountain and seascape, the onward way can be chosen from a number of different routes. For a quick return to the Glencoe road one can follow the ridge down west and then south until an easy descent can be made into the coire. Here a path will be found that will deposit one on the valley floor near Achnam-beithach.   Alternatively the ridge to Stob Coire nan Lochan can be taken.   This has the advantage of giving the traveller (if he is that type) a chance of 'bagging' another top, as well as affording him the opportunity of viewing the short but steep cliffs of the Coire.   They hold two of the Glen's classic winter climbs — Twisting Gully and S.C. Gully.

From the summit of Stob Coir there is, once again, a choice of how to proceed.

The ridge to the west and north can be taken along the top of the cliffs until an easy descent to the tiny lochans can be made.   From there an easy but steep descent is made to the floor of the Glen by a path on the Gearr Anoch side of the coire.   However, a descent of the east ridge of Stob Coire allows the opportunity to visit another of Glencoe's places of interest — the Lost Valley.   From the low point on the ridge, before it continues along Gearr Anoch, a descent in a south-easterly direction can be made.   This is done to avoid the cliffs on the east face of Gearr Anoch.   Eventually a path is reached which leads directly down to the Lost Valley.   It is a wonderfully atmos-pheric place: in summer a fine green meadow surrounded by steep hills, and cut off physically and visually (hence its name) from Glencoe by the barrier of a huge primeval boulder field and narrow gorge.

While descending these, the visitor's eye will turn, not for the first time on his day's walk, to the notched ridge of the Anoch Eagach opposite.   This is another 'must' for the first time visitor, be it in summer or winter.   Usually the traverse is made from east to west, for this has the advantage of allowing a start of eight hundred feet above sea level.   Whichever way is chosen, there is invitably the boring walk back along the road after the climb.   The only way out of this difficulty, fantasised by many, but as far as can be ascertained, achieved by very few, is to organise two parties each with a car placed at opposite ends of the ridge.   Then when the parties meet on the ridge, the keys of the cars can be exchanged.

Enough of complex logistics. The first problem that confronts the Ridge team is summoning sufficient energy to climb the seemingly endless slopes of Am Bodach. This can be done directly, though some may prefer to avoid the steep, broken part of the hill by traversing under the first large rock face encountered into the coire on the right. This may be the preferred way in winter.

After lingering (a euphemism for recouping one's strength after the ascent) on the summit admiring the view of Bidean and the superb gullies that shoot down to Glencoe, a descent from Am Bodach is made. In winter this can look alarming; but by using the diagonal weaknesses it is achieved with relative ease, and soon the next main summit is attained. Now the entertainment really begins, for the famous pinnacles have to be negotiated. This is fairly easy in summer as the scratched and worn rock can be followed. In winter it is more difficult. However, proper winter climbing equipment, an ice axe and crampons, and the knowledge of how to use them, will ease the way to broader, safer ridge-walking.

As all good guidebook readers will know, it is dangerous to attempt a descent into Glencoe before reaching the final peak, Sgur nam Fiannaidh. Too many people have got themselves into serious trouble and some have died doing that. It is better to enjoy the high country for a little longer, and perhaps experience a winter sunset over the beautiful seascape below. From the final summit, a descent can be made down the right hand side of Clachaig Gully, where there is a dreadfully eroded path. Care must be taken even here, especially in the winter, for a slip into the Gully would be disastrous. That too has happened.

It seems almost superfluous to recommend Glencoe to the reader for it is obvious that the place is well known and popular. The tents perpetually clustered around the Clachaig and the growing problems of erosion on some of the more popular ascents bear eloquent witness to this. However, if you have not been there, go, and soon. The place is magnificent. As a superb concentration of high hills and ridges, hidden corries and great climbs combined with ease of access, it is unrivalled in mainland Britain.

Of course, nowadays things will be different, but it is not the purpose of this book to comment on the quality of life for climbers in Glencoe today. It is dangerous for those of yesteryear, in looking for their lost youth, to lament that things are no longer as they were. They can never be sure whether, in the sophistication and change of taste occasioned by advancing years, it is they, and not the place, that has changed. Behaviour and stories that once delighted and amazed may now appear mundane, immature and boring. And so the present generation may well have their own adventures, heroes and character that go unseen by the ageing, jaded eyes.

Yet there is a strong impression that things are very different today, for there have been a number of changes that have led to a greater fragmentation and a loss of characters among climbers. The most obvious of these changes is the huge increase in the numbers involved. Climbing is a booming sport made popular by television spectaculars, school outdoor programmes and perhaps most significant of all, the development of good protection that makes life at the top a lot safer. At one time everybody knew everybody else. Now there are so many that it's impossible. Then there is the loss of Cameron's Barn, the last open and free doss in Glencoe. With it has gone the opportunity to meet others from different groups and ways of life. Similarly, methods of transport have changed. Whereas at one time club buses and even hitch-hiking provided social contact with others, the increased use of cars has served to isolate one group from another.

Moreover the 'great proletarian revolution' is over, and while it is obvious that many climbers are still working class, the impression is that the middle classes have reasserted themselves in terms of numbers and influence. Why this should be is unclear, but it is perhaps related to the fact that climbing places increasing emphasis on expensive equipment, and thus has become a sport for the relatively well-to-do. Also with the extinction of club buses, climbers must now have cars or go through the agonies of hitchhiking, an option, judging from the few who do it, rejected by the majority.

Along with the dominance of the middle class inevitably comes a tendency towards blandness. Gone to a large extent are the characters whose anarchistic life style and quick wits were manufactured along with the ships they built in John Brown's, Connel's and Stephen's. For that matter, gone also are the ship yards and factories that produced those men. The men have been replaced on the hills: nothing has replaced the environment that produced them. The iron men have been replaced by teachers and computer programmers whose life and different world view is manifested in different attitudes to climbing. The old Creagh Dhu had an outlook that was not dissimilar to that of the aristocracy of England. One was serious about one's sport but one did not have to try to be superior. One simply *was* superior! Thus 'gentleman' amateurs were always expected to beat the professional, be it at cricket, rugger or soccer. It was not a question of tactics or training but of breeding. Similarly with the Creag Dhu, the attitude appeared casual, difficulties were understated, nobody trained and latterly some drank and smoked more than was probably good for them. Today the seriousness of the *petit bourgeois* in climbing is crudely overt. Vast amounts of equipment, including the abominable and increasingly ubiquitous chalk are used. The winter is spent training on climbing walls and doing press-ups. Leading climbers are seen in the Kingshouse drinking orange juice. All they ever talk about is climbing. No doubt standards have improved and harder climbs are being done by more people, yet one cannot help feel the loss of the Tams and all the Willies.

The Tarf Hotel

DREADFUL DOSSES

The designs of nature, those of the Highland latifundi, and those of mountaineers, do not always coincide. The old estate buildings which today are used as bothies, were built to be near grouse-moors, deer forests, sheep grazings or forestry works, not as shelter for future generations of climbers. Thus it happened that many bothies were in less spectacular, and hence less visited, parts of the Highlands. The northern Grampians, south of the Cairngorms, abounded in open bothies in the 1950s and 1960s. But those tended to be the ones that no-one bothered to maintain, with the result that they are, sadly, falling away. Even in the 1960s, ruins existed not only of the infamous period of the Clearances, but also of the dwellings built to replace them. Some of those deserve to be preserved in print, even if the stonework has crumbled away.

Corienalarig is, or was, a bothy in a dreary and unlovely situation. About 5 miles south of Braemar, it lies in north-facing Glen Clunie, 'The Land of Perpetual Shadows', where the sun never shines, the sky always seems leaden and the rounded hills drained of colour. Why it became a well-frequented doss is difficult to say — there was nothing to climb in the area, and little to look at. Its saving graces were that it was a mere half mile from the road, and that firewood was plentiful. The bothy has probably gone the way of all flesh by now, since in the mid-1960s the roof had crashed in on one half of the building, and much of the lath and floorboards were disappearing 'up the lum'. It was the only bothy with a picture gallery. One of its plaster walls had been adorned with a huge charcoal mural of the bothy and the surrounding hills. Admired by all, it nevertheless gave rise to weird feelings. There was something strange about it, and in the flickering firelight, the trees seemed to sough in the wind.......

99

Since there was nothing to do at Corienalarig, an early resort to the cameraderie of the fireside was the usual answer. After the usual moaning questions about why we had come there, the lighter moments of tale-telling would begin. The time when Stumpy's sleeping place — a rickety table — collapsed under him, would be relived, and the time when Mealie's glasses were knocked off by flying cow sharn used as a rounders ball. Then there was the great salmon chase in the nearbye river. Trapped in a deep pool, the fish narrowly escaped death by stoning, spearing and every other form of mortality thought up by desperate men. They failed, and that night it was again sardines for tea, and the thought of what might have been. But as the sky darkened and the fire flickered, the talk inevitably turned to mattters less substantive. One one occasion, three companions were seated round the fire. One had told the story of the Gelder Ghost, to which the second had replied with that of the Callater poltergeist.

Now, the third person was an easily-impressed, highly-strung fellow, the said Mealie of the Sharn. In the gathering darkness he began to look nervously over his shoulder at the dark corners of the bothy, and then back to the security of the fire, to the great amusement of Stumpy and the tale-teller.

The wind was rising. Loose doors and windows rattled — or were they tried by unseen hands? As the temperature fell, the wood began to shrink and creak — or was it being trodden by unseen feet? A larger than usual gust led to a scraping, rolling noise upstairs. Seeing that Mealie was visibily shaken by this, his companion whispered as if in fear (though he thought he knew), 'Fit's that?' Then the noise was repeated, but louder, and seizing the opportunity of devilment he suggested, in mock trembling tones, 'Something's upstairs!' Mealie was now rigid with fear, unable to do more than utter a low, whining laugh. In triumph the torturer turned to Stumpy, to share his pleasure, but started back. There Stumpy sat, mouth moving soundlessly, eyes dilated with the whites showing clearly in the half light. Hilarity turned to hysteria: he was now alone with a pair turned irrational with fear, and capable of panic. Lamely he added, 'It's only the cans we were chucking through the skylight the day.'

But in the silence that followed, even his conviction drained away. The wind howled, and up above the scraping, and what seemed like soft treading, belied his words. Desperation led to courage. A proposal to mount an investigation seemed to lessen the paralysis which had overtaken the party. Ice axes were handed round and candles carried high. At the door a mad scramble not to be first out halted progress, but then, grasping each other for grim death, the corridor was gained. Instantly the candles blew out and the trio were swamped by darkness. After much stumbling, the stair was reached and ascended by touch. Eyes were becoming adjusted to the dark, and some moonlight was illuminating the upstairs room when the axe-wielding band gained entry.

Everywhere lay empty cans, lobbed through the skylight window for sport during the dull day. As the wind howled through the empty window frame, the cans rolled around the floor. The source of the noise now revealed, the party worked frantically to clear the room, lobbing the cans back out through the skylight. As the last one vanished, a cloud covered the moon and panic again took control. Axes were abandoned, and each leapt for the safety of the stairs, trampling mates as they fled. The door to the lower room was gained, but would not open.

'It's inside! It's inside!' gibbered Mealie.

And watched terrified as the door swung open in answer to his words. The fire light helped sanity to return, and as the trio stood stock still, Stumpy realised he'd been trying to pull the door instead of push it. The forbidding threshold was then crossed. Once inside, the door was barricaded, and an emotionally exhausted party watched the fire slowly dying.

'We've left our axes outside,' said one.

'Leave them there,' was the reply.

Silence fell. Then the wind rose again, and above their heads the scraping began once more. They exchanged looks, but did not speak. It was a long night, and in the brave light of morning, investigation revealed that all the cans had been removed in the sortie. But the rolling and scraping had not stopped.

Though no-one could explain why Corienlarig became popular, there is no mystery in why it ceased to be so.

Corienlarig is not the only dreadful doss in that part of the hills. They are many. But if you were to have conducted a poll in the 1960s on the most dreadful doss, few bothiers would have opted for other than Callater. The lower reaches of Glen Callater are quite pleasant, but around the bothy it is dreary in the extreme, and the loch beside it is an insipid stretch of water. From Callater most of the country is dull, except for the small and exquisite Corrie Kander, where there always used to be an eyrie. The Lodge itself is a squat, dull building, and the bothy is unfit for human habitation. Actually, there are two options, equally dreadful. One was an outhouse full of cans, implements and rubbish. Once a group slept in it, unpacking in the dark and wondering about the funny smell. In the morning they awoke to find deer carcases suspended above them, and the floor filthy with blood and entrails. It obviously doubled as a deer larder.

The usual bothy was the old stables opposite, occasionally still used for ponies, and of course full of dung when the ponies were there. There was no fixed door, only a loose one laid over the gap, and the roof was well past its best. It seemed to have marvellous powers, and pundits asserted that it rained or snowed heavier inside the doss than outside. The floor was always wet, and to complete the picture of misery, there was no fire. On occasion, desperation caused climbers to break into the lodge, via an easily forced skylight window, and a dangling drop. The problem was in getting out again. You had to get your gear through the skylight, and then pull yourself through by main force.

Two mountaineers, men whose integrity was as pure as the driven slush, used to tell of how they had entered the Lodge thus, and unpacked in the darkness to repose. On lying down to rest, one of them felt a heavy blow in the back.

'What the......did ye dae that for?' he cried.

'Dae fit?' replied the other, and on being told, denied the crime. Mollified, repose was resumed, but the iritation continued in the form of a slap on the face. A set-to and threatened fisticuffs resulted, then the aggrieved party finally moved to the other side of the room. In transit, a mighty push sent him flying. On leaping towards his pal, he found him abed, and still. Imagination began to take control. The sleeping bag he was carrying went through the skylight, and he followed, leaping for the lintel and swinging his legs to gain momentum. Something grabbed at his feet. He tumbled outside, jumped from the roof, and fled to the safety of the stables, where he spent an unquiet night.

In the morning his refreshed pal emerged, and listened to his tale. 'Sounds like a poltergeist,' was his considered verdict. The victim's doubts may not have totally vanished, but he was prepared to trade them for the kudos he attained in other dosses and in pubs, by retelling the tale. And Callater Lodge's reputation was made.

Adversity does not always bring out the best in people. The middle class 'Outward Bound' school of philosophy, or the older working class 'we were poor but we were happy' tradition of talking, both rely heavily on the idea that conflict with the elements and with one's weaknesses reveals a person's latent virtues, and unites him with his comrades in deep fraternity. One reads the tales of bygone days with wonder; under the widening horizons conflict is never encountered. Can it really have been like that? Cameraderie certainly existed, but when Patey writes that: *'All the bothies were well patronised... At one and all you would be assured of a friendly welcome round the fire in the evening....formal introductions were unnecessary.'* (One Man's Mountains), surely at least in part this represents middle aged nostalgia for lost youth? Mountaineers are no more perfect than other mortals, and the pressure of circumstances can reveal the unpleasant, as well as the pleasant, sides of their characters.

It was a snowy night, and the path was hard going as four mountaineers made their way towards Callater. Spirits were low. Their original aim had been abandoned because the weather was impossible. Callater was of easier access. On they trudged, packs laden with heavy climbing gear (which was useless at Callater), grumbling and ill-tempered. It was very cold, and a comfortless night was expected at the bothy. As they neared the doss, in a sudden burst of energy following a hushed confab, two of the party, led by Desperate Dan, separated themselves from the others, and sped bothy-wards. On reaching the doss, it was found to be completely filled with snow. But Dan knew what he was about. There was a door in the doss, detached, that served as a sleeping platform. Digging this out before the others came, he and his accomplice prepared to use it atop the snow, as insulation against cold and damp. As this act was being perpetrated, the others arrived. They were tired, and anticipating a night of misery, hence were in no mood for niceties.

Spotting the door, one of them, piqued now that the reason for the race to the bothy was clear, proposed: 'We'll use the door. You lads have your under-mattresses.' These were scarce, new-fangled innovations at the time, scorned by habitual bothiers. If the owners of those had used them, plus bivvy sheets as undercover, all would have been assured of a reasonably comfortable night. Dan did not see it like that, and applied his logical powers to rebut such an argument.

'We got here first, and it should be ours. The fact that we've also got under-blankets is beside the point. We carried them in for our own comfort.'

Dan then called upon his partner to complete their preparations, and he, somewhat shamefacedly, moved to help. Whereupon the rival party stood atop the door and announced:

'We're taking it. You can't expect your mates to sleep in the snow while you are comfortable!'

With determined and self-righteous postures being adopted on both sides, things were looking grim. Tempers were frayed and violence a possibility. But Dan's partner Stumpy, in an unusual outburst of decisiveness, stated 'Let them hae it,' and an ice axe battle to the death was avoided. Not a word was spoken as the party — now decisively two parties — retired to separate horse stalls for the night, out of sight of each other, and nursing their mutual resentment.

In the morning, after repose and warmth had restored spirits, all four were shamefaced, and went about their business, carefully avoiding all reference to the 'Battle of the Door'. That night, as they retired, Dan said audibly to his companion: 'These under-mattresses are great. They're all you need, even on snow.' After a suitable pause, from over the partition, the victorious party in the battle added: 'This f------door is a waste of time. It's as hard as nails, and the moulding digs into your back.' Silence fell: peace was made.

Altanour figures as a bothy in past accounts of Cairngorm mountain life. But for many years past, it has been a skeleton of a building, surrounded by its clump of dying trees. Rumour always had it that there remained a cellar suitable for use under the building, long after the Lodge had fallen into ruins. And to investigate this cellar, and seek adventure, a duo, trusting in rumour, set out in times long past.

Glen Ey runs southwards from the village of Inverey, where stands a monument to its most famous son, Lamont, the 19th century Astonomer Royal of Bavaria. Many left the glen for less exalted destinations, such as the 40-odd families who were cleared to make way for sheep in the 1840s. The last inhabited house in Glen Ey was the shepherd's cottage at Auchelie, now boarded up and abandoned.

The Glen walk is a delightful one, with constantly changing views of river and trees in its lower reaches, becoming wilder where the river bends to show the Hills of Hell (Ben Iutharn) in the distance. The object of the expedition was to bivouac at Altanour and cross the Hills of Hell to the tantalising Fealar Lodge lying in their shadow. They never made Fealar Lodge, and here is the reason why.

The day started well enough, but as Auchelie was passed, the weather turned foul. Sleeting rain began to fall, further wetting ground already sodden from melting snow. Halfway up the glen lies a wooden hut, about 4 feet square and about the same height. They sped past this to gain the shelter of Altanour. It did not look too promising from a distance, and seemed little more than a heap of rubble with a gaunt gable end. And that is what it was. The walls had caved inwards, and if ever there had been a cellar, it would take more than their weak hands to remove the tons of rubble covering it. It was wet, it was windy, it was cold, and it was getting dark.

'The hut,' suggested Stumpy, in a flash of genius.

Seconds later, they were pounding back down the glen, spirits raised and backs to the wind. They arrived at it footsore (Braemar to Altanour is 12 miles, and they had retraced the last three). They were in that euphoric and usually illusory state caused by feeling that all troubles are over. They had, of course, just begun. There was a sort of door to the construction, but it had been left open, and the hut was filled with drifted snow to the depth of a foot or more. But it was the only available shelter, so in they got. Then the agony really began. The cold penetrated through sleeping bags and into aching limbs. The heat of bodies melted the snow, which refroze, forming cases of ice round bodies. On turning, it was difficult to fit back into the melted-out hollows. In addition they gained an insight into the medieval torture of 'Little Ease', where prisoners were confined in cells too short to stretch out in. Legs had to remain permanently bent, or be stretched up walls, to fit the hut. A long and miserable night eventually passed, and they rose at the first glimmering of dawn. The quest was abandoned, and they crossed the hills to Corienlarig, where at least a fire — and circulation — could be got going. From this episode developed a paranoia about bothies known only by hearsay. Frantic checking and quizzing to establish their existence in advance have ensured that the drama of Altanour has not been repeated. There are things you can live without.

Some bothies function as mental frontier posts. To the Aberdonian, you could say that the Shelter Stone and Corrour marked the limits of his *patria chica* to the north and west (the hills beyond being too far to visit in a weekend.) To the south and west, the forts of the Maginot Line protecting him from the broad and alien world used to be the Geldie, the Bynack bothies, and that disputed no-mans-land, the Tarf Hotel. Alas, all of these have either crumbled and vanished, or are set to do so, unless major renovations are carried out on them. The Geldie in its day, for example, must have been a princely establishment, though today it is virtually a total ruin. A large-scale shooting lodge, it lay in the less frequented pass from Braemar to Aviemore via the White Bridge and Glen Feshie.

But already in the mid-1960s the lower floor was totally in ruins, although acess could still be gained to the upper floor by a rickety staircase. It was only used once by acquaintances who shall be nameless, when the trial marker poles were uprooted, and Geldie gained a huge charcoal slogan **Doon wi the Feshie Road.** Such a road would have split in two the largest area of wilderness in Scotland, and was thankfully abandoned.

Nearbye lay Bynack Lodge, on the road through to Blair Atholl by the Tilt, another bothy in living memory, though already a ruin by the 60s. A heap of stones always known as such has not the same capacity to arouse emotion as one which was known as a shelter, and where time was passed round a convivial fire. Near to Bynack stood Ruigh nan Clach, still an excellent bothy 20 years ago though little used, as it was far from any major hills. Only vacated at the end of W.W.II, it had stood up well since then, and still had odd items of furniture. Fishgut Mac once met a man in a Braemar pub, tears in his eyes, who said he had been born there, and that his father was a native Gaelic speaker.

It was a pleasant walk in from the White Bridge to the Clach, but for all that it could be gone now, as 20 years have passed since the writer set eyes on it.

One day a duo did the circuit of Beinn Bhrotain from Ruigh nan

Clach. They went like steam engines till they attained the fence surrounding the bothy. The stop there was fatal, and exhaustion took over. In the lovely evening they sat watching the sun sink, on their backs in the grass, and too tired to move on. Later, when they crawled the last 50 yards, had a fortifying meal and went for an evening stroll up the burn, 'The peace that passeth all understanding' was rudely shattered when they found a dead sheep smack in the middle of the water supply they had just cooked with. Despite its state of decomposition, they lived to tell the tale many times, and put greenhorns off their grub. It was most effective told at mealtimes.

On visits to those dreadful dosses, they often heard of a fabled bothy deep in the hills where few had trod. This was the Tarf Bothy. The Tarf ranks with Faindouran as the remotest bothy in Scotland; it is a full 15 miles walk from Blair Atholl, and not much less from the Linn o' Dee. It lies on a high pleateau, five miles west of the Bedford Memorial Bridge, surrounded by what look like low hills, but are in fact the tops of Munroes. Hearing that it was in a bad way, and wishing to see it before it vanished, a mountaineer set off on a journey of homage. Even on a sentimental pilgrimage, it is a long hard walk to the Tarf with a pack. As dusk began falling, and the bothy was nowhere in sight, old doubts about its existence began to surface. He also glanced nervously at the Tarf, rising with the melting snow, and recalled the cautionary tale of a friend, who had been trapped on the wrong side of the Tarf, and forced to retreat to the Bedford Bridge to cross. By then darkness forced them back to Blair Atholl, and necessitated a return trip to the bothy to collect gear the next day.

But there it was; rusted red roof standing out even in the falling light. Steps were quickened and the doss attained. The reason for its name soon became apparent. Some wit had carried up a couple of A.A. metal signs, announcing that the said establishment was a three star one, and fixed them to the wall. It may well have been in its day, with 5 large rooms, plumbing and the remains of a hot water system, whose old boiler rusted away behind the doss. But the Tarf Hotel's days of glory are now gone. All the rooms bar one were missing their walls or roofs, while floors and lath had been ripped out for firewood. The remaining habitable room had a fireplace and two spring beds, as well as table and chairs, but the ceiling oozed water from the damaged roof. There was no hut book in the bothy, nor sign of recent occupation. Apparently it was little used, and less maintained. As he left next day to climb Cairn a' Chlamain and return home, he felt he had seen the Tarf for the first and last time: another couple of winters and it would be no more.

One doss which has long gone, though the building remains, was in Inverey, 6 miles west of Braemar village, where the bus went to in days of fable and faery. This village was the last surviving Gaelic community in Aberdeenshire, but went into steady decline after W.W. II. By the mid-60s most houses were deserted and derelict. Today they are holiday homes. There had for a long time been an open doss in Inverey, named after its proprietor, Ma Gibbs. Here for a small fee climbers out from Aberdeen could sleep in her barn. Apparently she was continuing a long-estabished Inverey tradition. One of the first village inhabitants, when Glen Ey was cleared, was Maggie Gruer, who maintained an open bothy in the village before W.W.II

Part of the attraction of staying at Inverey was the fact that Mar Lodge, with its bar and Saturday late night dance, lay just across the river. Mountaineers 20 years ago were not renowned for their success with the fair sex. Today expensively clad sveldt young damsels seem to hang on to every word uttered by mountaineering Adonises with their modulated accents. But the nearest your working class misfits of the 60s got to the opposite sex — apart from the recurring fantasy that the bothy would be hoaching with women — was Mar Lodge on a Saturday night. Here, too, fantasy largely replaced fact. Long before Gay Bars were common, Mar Lodge had single-sex dances largely by default. There were very few of the opposite sex there, and those few were generally 'boxed in'. There were no lusty Amazons or peasant wenches to be seen.

The band put a final damper on things. Three old fogeys in dickey suits, scraping away at a fiddle, cello and piano, with atrocious renditions of the *Blue Danube* or some other tune straight out of Victor Sylvester, when even Aberdeen had heard of the Beatles by then..... We all believed then that the reason Mar Lodge held the dance was to obtain a late licence, and make a fortune out of the mountaineers as their fantasies crumbled, and they took refuge in drink. There they stood, staring bemusedly at the band or shuffling in hairy socks to the bar, the last word in sartorial elegance and smooth dance floor technique. No-one ever danced; no-one ever even tried.

And then there was the river. In the early evening, the mile and a half walk to the Lodge was pleasant enough. The worse for drink, and disappointed in amorous intentions, the option generally chosen at night was to go straight across the river. Apparently there was once a ford to Inverey, and many a mountaineer got a good soaking looking for it. The best plan, if the river was low, was simply to make a dash for it and hope for the best. If it was in spate, there was the problem of trying to divide the party into trios, and executing the prescribed method of crossing a river safely, by circular motions. Generally, these attempts looked more like ball room dancing than anything that happened in Mar Lodge, and usually ended in a panic flight in mid stream.

Philistine youth never paid much note to someone like Ma Gibbs, and that now seems a great loss. For the Gibbs and Gruers, peasants who offered bothy accomodation to climbers, have gone, and gone for ever, from the Cairngorms and elsewhere. And Inverey, which had once echoed to the play of Gaelic infants, is now polluted for a few months each year by the clipped and impeccable accents of the spoiled brats of suburbia.

These southern bothies were, as mentioned, generally in quite unspectacular country, but they had a place in all our affections nevertheless. Most of them were sought out, found and tested, and then passed on by word of mouth. Their users did not discover them first, but rediscovered them themselves. Today they are falling into

110

ruin, and open mountain shelters in Scotland are becoming fewer. The old spectrum of everything from luxury to Little Ease has gone, and with it the uncertainties of search. Soon, only the MBA-maintained bothies will remain, and the novice will work through them, like a hosteller through his SYHA book. Such an outcome is inevitable, and the only alternative to the collapse of all bothies. But sadness and nostalgia remains for the days when bothies were hunted out from dots on the map, and passed on by word of mouth. Future generations cannot have that bittersweet feeling, of being the tailend of a chapter in mountain history. Possibly those dreadful dosses are already gone. But even if they still existed, and were visited again, it could not be as it was in the days of Mealy Pudding and Fishgut Mac.

On The Skye Ridge

SKYE

Getting to Skye was always a problem. Hitch-hiking in high summer was murder, and people used to spend valuable days of precious short holidays standing rooted in some God-forsaken spot like Crianlarich or, worse, Tyndrum, soaked or sweating, but invariably being driven near demented by the ubiquitous midges. There was also the risk of being forced to hold daft conversations with American hitch-hikers. 'I was at your Bal-mo-ral. I loved your Queen.'

Frustrated by his lack of progress, the Skye-bound mountaineer was usually not in the mood to be gracious to the naive visitor who trampled around the pronunciation of beloved place names. So the poor American found himself gruffly dismissed up the road with a curt: 'She's no' ma Queen, pal.'

The root of this lack of mobility lay in the fact that in high summer most of the cars to which our heroes extended their hopeful thumbs were full of people going on their holidays. The road was jammed with convoys of old, overloaded bangers, polythene flapping over ancient suitcases on the roof, and maw, paw, granny, the weans and a big dog, their blank faces filling every window, waving idiotically to the kerb-bound, would-be traveller.

Even if transport was arranged, there were dangers, and on the Glasgow Fair Friday the knowledgeable onlooker could discern the young and foolish mountaineer lurch from a pub on the Great Western Road into the glare of the early evening sun. High in spirits not only of the psychological variety, such a fellow was likely to have a problem, for although he was off on the most important holiday of his so-far brief climbing career, he had left most of his meagre supply of money behind the bar. He would have plenty of time next day to contemplate his youthful indiscretion, for he faced a long journey, ill with a monumental hangover, in the bouncing back of the van as it made its slow and intermittent progress down the single lane track of asphalt that masqueraded as the road from Glen Shiel to Kyle. But that evening he would have the more pressing problem of trying to curb the more idological excesses of Tam, excesses which manifested themselves in his own peculiar brand of class-warfare — the throwing of empty screw-tops (beer bottles) at any car that was big enough to belong to what Tam called *the bourgeoisie*. Luckily, he, too, was over-refreshed, and always failed to make a hit

For such a traveller to arrive in Skye was always better than travelling in hope. (Although, as the reader will have guessed, hope was not a typical emotion experienced by the average hitch-hiker.) However, the frustrations and problems of the journey would soon be forgotten, for coming over the shoulder of the northern ridge that forms Glenbrittle the mist could suddenly clear and the traveller, no matter how many times he had previously made the passage, would be forced to stop. He had already passed Sligachan and gazed in awe at that most beautiful of peaks, Sgurr nan Gillean, but this is something special. Here a great stretch of the ragged ridge is revealed to give the visitor a most dramatic impression of the scale of the place. On his left is Bruach na Frithe, whose grassy ridge from Tobar nan Vais-lean gives the walker the easiest place of access to a Black Cuillin summit. What a contrast that easy-angled slope is to the notched and airy summits of Sgurr a Mhadaidh, a favourite traverse of climbers and walkers. As the eye descends from those great summits, it is caught by the complex double corries of Tairneilear and Coir' a' Mhadaidh, which are separated by the conspicuous promontory of Sgurr an Fheadain, whose outstanding feature is the great defile of the Water-pipe Gully.

In the early sixties, many of those who stopped at that vantage point were lads from Glasgow. The Cuillins had a magical attraction, and although in later years many were to spend summers in the Alps, at that time money and time off work made Skye the place to spend the Glasgow Fair (holiday) fortnight. Everybody who normally spent their weekends at Glencoe would congregate down at the campsite at the black beach in Glenbrittle. Nowadays, if you go there you will find a multi-coloured tented city, serviced by toilets and a shop, and with rules about noise and fires. In those days, it was wild and free. No toilets, no rules and no warden. Just people out to enjoy themselves climbing, meeting for a bit of 'patter' round the fire and going to ceilidhs in the nearby villages.

Those ceilidhs could be pretty wild affairs. Once a crowd of the lads from Glenbrittle hitch-hiked to Portree for one, and it turned out to be a disaster, for among that group was Charlie. Charlie was a young Clydeside shipyard worker who appeared to be a very quiet and gentle man. However, it was at that ceilidh his friends were to discover that Charlie possessed a little flaw of character, something that was to manifest itself again on a number of occasions before he finally departed from the climbing scene. You see, Charlie, at that stage in his life, was not so much interested in dancing as he was in trying to pick a fight with the biggest guy in the place. This was not the product of some deep-rooted psychological disorder, but merely the expression of a complaint common to a number of young, male working class Glaswegians. He wanted to demonstrate his masculinity, and not being a coward, he chose not to waste his time on the small fry.

In Portree, he picked a monster. All shoulders, muscular arms and big red beard. Once he had selected his challenge (it would be wrong to call his opponent a victim for usually Charlie picked up most of the penalty points), Charlie would stalk him around the floor until a suitable moment presented itself for the confrontation. On this occasion Charlie followed the big guy into the toilet whereupon, after a brief exchange of insults and threats, the scuffling began. What followed was not expected by Charlie. Onlookers, locals and visitors, instead of trying to separate the combatants, they all joined

115

in. It was like one of those John Wayne movies in which everybody joins in the bar-room brawl, for soon the small toilet was full of guys punching and wrestling.

The noise produced by this melee soon attracted Charlie's friends and the action they took was both sensible and timely. Sensible because they dragged him out of the battle in which he was not doing very well, and timely because just as they emerged the local police were arriving to deal with the fracas that was still merrily continuing.

'Where's the man that started this?' asked the sergeant.

'He's still in there,' replied one of Charlie's friends, pointing to the toilet.

As the police fought their way in there, the lads headed first for the door and then for Glenbrittle. The first target was more easily achieved than the second, for, fearing that the police, on discovering the real cause of the disturbance, would give chase, not only could the lads not hitch hike, but they had to jump into the moor and hide every time a car's headlights pierced the darkness behind them.

It is a long way from Portree to Glenbrittle, about twelve miles, and it was well after sunrise before the long distance merry- makers staggered, exhausted, into the campsite. An onlooker, noting the heather that had attached itself to their clothing during their reluctant leaps into the moor, remarked to them: 'I thought you crowd were at the dancing. Where did they hold it? In a bog?'

The lads, of course, did not appreciate such wit or the unintended pun, and all that merry quipper got for his troubles was a series of hostile looks from tired and hungry men who longed only for their food and sleeping bags.

The climbing was of course, despite the occasional dissipations of the visitors, the main attraction, for Skye is a real paradise for climbers. In the popular Coir Lagan, for example, there is an unrivalled collection of long and short climbs of every standard. But the unique appeal of the Black Cuillin lies in its magnificent ridge which offers superb, though relatively untaxing days, such as the round of Coire Lagan, as well as one of the most splendid of British mountaineering experiences, the traverse of the complete ridge. All this is set in a beautiful combination of high rocks and seascape. In one's memory the bad times tend to erode quickly, with the result that nostalgia invariably consists of pleasures like the contentment one feels after a great climb, sitting on some high spot, lazily watching a couple of yachts drift slowly towards Rhum on a dazzling sea.

Reality, unfortunately, was often somewhat different, and the weather in Skye can be unkind. More often than he would like to remember, the climber standing on the beach was presented with the dismal sight of the corries filled with black clouds, over which would be washing diagonal walls of very solid-looking rain. It was on such a day that two raw seventeen-year olds, fired by tales from Bell and Murray, set out to discover the great mysteries of which they had read. Their target was the famous slab and Cioch of Sron na Ciche in Corrie Lagan, and although they had neither much experience nor equipment —a rope, three slings and three huge Stubai screwgate carabiners, all borrowed from the Langside M.C. —they chose to achieve this modest ambition by climbing the Cioch West route.

It was not long before they regretted that decision, for on the first pitch the lad who was brave or foolish enough (even he was not sure which) to go first was soon in difficulty. He had heard all about the rough and adhesive qualities of gabbro. It would take the skin off an elephant's bum — wasn't that what the old timer (who was probably all of twenty-three) had said?. Yet here he was in a horrible, wet chimney, his big, bendy boots sliding about on rock that looked more like coal than the black sandpaper he had been led to expect. And there was the ground, far below. Funny, he thought, how it does not look so high when you're standing on the ground looking up. Later, he was to learn that his mountaineering mentors had omitted to inform him of a little variation to be found in the gabbro which is not always obliging to the climber. This was basalt, a form of rock very different from the gabbro, for being sleek and slippy, especially when wet, it had few of the predominant rock's qualities.

117

However at that stage of his short climbing career he was not interested in the geological niceties of the Black Cuillin. His problem was more immediate, for his legs were beginning to shake and he was thinking he might soon involuntarily join his anxious companion below. He would have to make a move, hopefully upwards. To achieve this he jammed as much of himself as he could into a crack on his left and climbed his heaving way on to easier ground above. After that it was all relatively straight forward, although, if he were to be honest, the feelings of desperation experienced below, returned once again, albeit briefly, on beginning the airy traverse that constitutes a famous passage of this climb.

Eventually, weary, wet, and a bit wiser, the bold twosome stood on the big terrace below the slab, staring in awe at the great Cioch. Sure, they thought, they had been around a bit. Only last weekend they had seen and climbed on the Rannoch Wall and hadn't they been to Ben 'An and the Whangie? But this was something else! The slab is only 200 feet high, but to the neophytes, uncomfortably aware of the 500 feet drop up which they had just struggled, it was huge. At the top of the right hand side of the slab was the Cioch, and from the angle from which they were looking, it forms a giant nose, audacious in its denial of gravity, its overhang making more gloomy an already gloomy day.

To reach the Cioch they would have to climb the slab. This they did on its extreme right hand side, and despite the streams of water up which they had to climb, they soon stood on top of that most remarkable lump of rock. Now, surely, they were real mountaineers! They had followed in the footsteps of the pioneers and were sitting where they had sat. All the rain in the world, most of which seemed to be going down their backs, could not dent their satisfaction.

The complacency nurtured by such sweet success was soon to be shattered. They were getting through their second Mars Bar, when their consciousness, so occupied with upward movement, began now to consider the hitherto unconsidered. How were they to get down again? One of them drew a soggy guidebook from deep within the recesses of equally soggy trousers. A quick consultation revealed that they had to climb down the route taken by Collie when he first climbed the Cioch. For the second time that day they had serious doubts about the integrity of those who praise gabbro. Cerainly this was gabbro, but so many people had passed this way, probably, like them, on the seat of their trousers, that it was extremely polished. That, combined with the fact that the slab was wet, gave the lads the impression that they were descending an ice rink set at approximately 40 degrees. The unease was not relieved by the drop into Eastern Gully on their right. Some penalty for a wee slip, that is, was the thought uppermost in their minds.

Situations like that invariably cause all but the most confident mountaineers to make small and tentative movements, and so they did. Nevertheless, they soon stood on the screes below the face. Tired and wet though they were, euphoria was to smooth their steps to the campsite below.

There was always a fire at night in the campsite, and people used to sit around and relate their adventures of that day or of days gone long before. Today, such things are frowned upon, and while it is true that fire making, if not carried out properly, can have a deleterious effect on a campsite, those people limited their fire to one spot and used only driftwood. That was until they burned the boat.

It was not a good, seaworthy boat. Its wooden structure, though covered in tar, was rotten with age and neglect. So long had it lain on the beach that the Black Cuillin sand had drifted through holes in its hull so as to embed it there permanently. It was obvious that it would never again feel the swell of the Minch beneath its keel.

The burning started casually enough. Just wee bits from the gunwales and thwarts to augment the driftwood. However, after a few nights of this its frame began to show. Then one night a large crowd was sitting round the fire when someone mentioned that the ribs of the boat were showing, and that the owner, if anyone owned or cared about such a hulk, might be annoyed. The answer to this dilemma was one of simple vandalism — destroy the evidence, burn the whole boat. The cry of assent from the gathered company had hardly died in the night air as they rushed to the boat and dragged it to the fire. It was like a dry land version of Uphellya. The rotten hull covered in tar burned so brightly that the occupants of nearby tents were able to read quite comfortably by the light.

The next morning the police arrived. A big sergeant and a young constable. Someone, then, did care about the boat, or perhaps it was only that the police wanted the law to be represented on a campsite that to them was as peaceful as Dawson City at the height of the gold rush. After going around the remnants of the fire with the toes of their boots, they made their way to the nearest tent, thinking, no doubt that there would be the culprits. As it happened, that tent was occupied by Black Rab. Now, Rab was a bit of a lad, whose name owed as much to some dark deeds as it did to his dark complexion and grubby appearance. He had seen a few things in his life, and was quick witted enough to make it unlikely that he would be intimidated by those two.

Rab was backing out of the tent on his hands and knees when the police arrived, and it was from that position he spotted their boots. He stood up, wiping his hands on his trousers, and looking as innocent as his shady appearance would allow, he nodded an acknowledgement to the arriving threat. The police did not waste any time with niceties.

'Who burned the boat?' asked the big sergeant, in his lilting West Highland accent.

'I dunno', replied Rab, and with a studied indifference born of other such interviews, he shrugged his shoulders.

'Ah-ah, I have you now', cried the big sergeant triumphantly. 'How did you know that the boat was burned?' To him, Rab had walked into the trap, admitting by inference that he was, at least, present when the damage was done. However, he had not reckoned on the speed of Rab's mind, for quick as a flash came the answer.

'You just told me'. Rab had heard this one before. As for the sergeant, he was flabbergasted. This stopped him dead in his tracks, and although he made threatening noises about taking Rab down to Portree and charging him that very minute, he did not come near him again. Rab was just one of those Glasgow hooligans anyway.

That was the end of the fires. The next year there were toilets and big signs warning of the dire consequences if fires were lit. That was a great pity, for fires were wonderfully communal affairs that brought the various groups together. There, drinking your tea, you met different people and listened to their fabulous tales. One memorable story heard there was about a lad who used to go away for weekends into the hills without socks.

He did not wear them in town either, and seemingly he once went into a shoe shop to buy shoes and the assistants thought they'd take a rise out of him.

'That's a rare pair of socks,' said one of them, winking at her mates. 'You'll no wear them out in a hurry.'

The lad looked at her innocently and replied, 'I don't know about that. I've got a vest and underpants of the same material and there's a hole in them already.'

In later years the camp lost much of its attraction. It was not only that it had become regimented. The company was no longer there, for by the mid sixties, the various groups were breaking up as fate and ambition took their tolls. Some met the women of their dreams and got married. Some have given up their wanderings and others have wandered away and have never wandered back. For the few that were left, alternative accommodation had to be found. One September, many years later, our two raw youths were not so raw, and along with a fellow Glaswegian and an Englishman they found on their travels (he had a car), they conned their way into the B.M.C. hut in Glenbrittle. It was a luxurious place with bunks, showers and electric rings. Far and away above the usual standard of howff to which those lads were accustomed. It was a perfect place from which to climb, and two of the team were keen to do just that. They had had a good summer in the Alps, and they were fit. So they

121

rushed out of the hut every morning and on to a hill. Al did not share their enthusiasm. He had had enough of climbing that year, and his mind was on other things. Portree was a 'hotspot' with still enough female tourists to make the ceilidhs seem very attractive.

So while his friends were out dicing with death on the slippery verticals, Al lay abed claiming illness. A strange illness it was, too, for around early evening the symptoms abated, and Al was out of his bunk and into his 'winkle-picker' shoes and Italian 'bum-freezer' jacket. With a quick comb of his wiry, embryonic Beatle haircut, he was out of the hut and into the Englishman's car, leaving behind only a dying echo of his whistled version of *She loves You*.

The interesting thing about all this was the warden's world view, which was such that she could not envisage that people in her hut could actually behave in this way. She was keen on the hills; everybody that came to her hut was keen on the hills, ergo Al must be keen on the hills. Thus when she found him in the kitchen at five in the morning, drunk, dressed in his winkle pickers and Italian jacket, noisily trying to assemble a post-ceilidh feast, she interpreted the scene in the context of her own particular *weltanschaung*, saying angrily to him: 'Just because you want to get up early to go climbing you don't have to waken the whole hut!

Al blinked uncomprehendingly at the retreating figure. 'What the hell was all that about?' he asked himself, not really expecting an answer.

Plans to climb at the north end of the ridge were always complicated by the fact that if one did not have a tent or could not afford to stay at the hotel, there was little in the way of accommodation around the Sligachan area. There was no real bothy there, and the bridges over what is now the old road did not afford the itinerant climber any comfort. The most famous of bothiers, Jock Nimlin, when denied the use of the bridges, hit upon an ingenious solution to the problem of dossing at Sligachan without a tent. He described in the B.B.C. Scotland Odyssey programme how he and a pal built a howfff out of a pair of builders' trestles and some building rubble found behind the hotel.

Later generations did not have to go to such lengths, for there used to be a wee hut out on the moor a short distance away from the hotel. It looked as if it had housed a small hydro electric generator or a watersupply system for there were old bits of machinery and a pipe that ran upstream into a weir on the burn. It was not comfortable, but it sufficed if nothing else was available — and nothing else was. Guests had to arrange themselves on the floor around the machinery when trying to sleep. Their discomfort was not relieved by the fact that the hut was a wee bit ramshackle, with no door and broken down walls and roof. It was a doss of a thousand draughts, unlikely, even had it survived, to have been sponsored by the M.B.A.

People using that hut could always seek some comfort in the public bar of the Sligachan Hotel. However, while it may be the case that today's climber will receive a warm welcome, in those days the Glasgow boys received, to say the least, a lukewarm welcome (with some justification, the reader might think, given the behaviour described in this book.) In the early sixties, the bar looked about as welcoming as a D.H.S.S. office, and was run by a female whose presbyterian philosphy of life did not include happiness in public bars. Not on Saturday nights, anyway. On one such night some of the lads were crowded into her establishment and they made the mistake of laughing at the tales told by a bard among them. She emerged to quieten them with a speech that reminded them of the proximity of the Sabbath, and silenced them with: 'There's too much la-ffing in here, anyway.'

Despite the then unwelcoming bar of the Sligachan Hotel, that end of the Cuillins is rich in attractions for the climber. From there one can ascend the fine and airy Pinnacle Ridge of Sgurr nan Gillean, before traversing west over a jumble of towers to the Basteir Tooth. One is also well placed for ascents of the Red Cuillin in general and Marsco in particular. That latter hill, positioned on the left side of the viewer standing at Slighachan, presents an interesting profile. A closer examination reveals a large rock amphitheatre bounded by a steep buttress of coarse red granophyre which gives a good climb of about 500 feet to an impressive hanging groove. The standard is about severe.

For the lads of the early sixties who are still around and active, Sligachan has become the place to stay. There are a number of reasons for this, of which the most important is the (to them) unacceptable situation at the campsite in Glenbrittle. However, recent visits have not produced anything like the events of their youth. Those were the products of pimply adolescence, the raucous clamourings of undiscovered manhood. Today, there is enjoyment of quieter things, of small groups, not large, of flowers and birds, not booze and birds. All that was fun, but now with the sober realisation of time's great gallop, there comes a concentration on corries undiscovered, climbs undone and summits not yet visited. Too soon their thoughts will echo the words of Louis MacNiece:

For now the time of gifts is gone —
O boys that grow, O snows that melt
O bathos that the years must fill.......

BEINN A BHUIRD AND THE SECRET HOWFF

Although a favourite amongst North-east climbers, Beinn a Bhuird, or the mountain of the tables, is rather neglected by the ordinary hill-goer. It does not even merit a mention in Poucher's *Scottish Peaks*, once the most-used hill-walkers' guide. This is possibly due to a combination of its extreme remoteness — it is at no point less than 10 miles from a public road — and to its unattractive appearance from such points (though the tantalising glimpse of Corrie na Ciche from Invercauld is an exception). This has kept the mountain less frequented than, for example, Lochnagar or Macdui, to the advantage of its quality of loneliness. Yet this is a pity, for Beinn a Bhuird is a fine mountain, some would say the finest of all the Cairngorm hills. Lochnagar boasts its north-east corrie, but Beinn a Bhuird is possessed of four magnificent rivals. These are the austere north-facing Garbh Chorrie, where snow lies late in the shadows, the small but superbly shaped Corrie na Ciche, and the two high corries of Dubh Lochan and nan Clach.

Another factor which may have deterred the hesitant could be the distinct lack of enthusiasm shown by the Invercauld Estate to mountaineers, some of whom imagine that a KEEP OUT sign represents something more than a landlord's delusions of grandeur, for there is no trespass law in Scotland. Few walkers up there have not had a run-in with the Invercauld gamies. But a major factor in the under-utilisation of the hill must have been the lack of obvious accommodation in its vicinity. It is not easily accessible from Braemar or Inverey, where there are youth hostels, and the only bothy in its lower reaches in Faindouran, and that is an epic 12 mile hike from the road end.

There is an open barn, sometimes cozy and hay-filled, just before Alltdourie Cottage, which has occasionally been used by those whose legs have given out, but stealth is required in its use. An alternative is to camp in the beautiful Fairy Glen, where the Slugain burn runs underground, and you lie on a verdant bed, listening to the invisible stream. This lies just east of Slugain Lodge, which Queen Victoria passed on her ascent of Beinn a Bhuird in 1850, and described as a 'very pretty little shooting box' (*Highland Journal*), but which is today a ruin. Pleasant scrambles can be had on Slugain slabs on an evening's stroll from the Fairy Glen. But it is an eerie place as the sun sinks westwards behind Slugain ruins, and one camper, claiming to have 'heard noises', abandoned his tent and fled to Invercauld in the gloaming, to return for it on the morrow. The ruins of Slugain offer enough shelter for the benighted in all but the worst of weathers, but little in the way of comfort.

But by far the best solution to the accommodation problem is one whose delights I will try to describe, but whose location I am not at liberty to divulge. The 'secret howff' of Beinn a Bhuird is a mystery that has miraculously been guarded for 30 years, the best kept secret in the history of Scottish mountaineering. The howff's location today is still tantalising those who know of its existence, but who have not been admitted to the word-of-mouth freemasonry which maintains its seclusion. There are even several imitation howffs in the vicinity, of inferior construction, which lure the curious into a false sense of discovery.

The history of the howff is itself shrouded in some obscurity. It was associated with the exploits of the late Tom Patey, who tells in his *One Man's Mountains* of this 'eighth wonder of the Cairngorms, with a stove, floor boards, genuine glass window and seating space for six' being constructed out of 'mighty beams of timber, sections of stove piping and sheets of corrugated iron' carried past the residence of the unsuspecting laird in the dead of night, by work parties out from Aberdeen, to a location virtually impossible to stumble on by accident or discover by design.   Patey gives 1954 as the date of its construct-ion, and the Kincorth Club as its builders.   The Club is gone, but the construction remains.   Some writers have made oblique references to the howff since then, but none, possibly fearing a visitation by a lynch party, has revealed its location.   It will be a crime if this rule is ever broken, a crime which many would rush to avenge.   Good luck to the hunter, but damnation to the publiciser!

No-one could ever forget their first trip to the 'Secret Howff', appetites doubtless whetted by the promise that this was something special, but ignorant of what to expect, except a long walk with pack from the road end.   Eventually, it is reached: built into the back of an outcrop, and sloping towards a lilliputian door, it is invisible from all but a restricted angle.   The walls, built from debris of the outcrop, blend into it, a perfect camouflage.   It is proof against the elements, crouching sheltered behind the rock, and built to last, being roofed, mortared and guttered to a competent standard.

Inside was an Aladdin's cave of delights.   Though the stove has been removed to give more space, and because of lack of fuel, it originally contributed to the antique-shop air.   On the wall hung an old clock.   On wet days climbers vented their frustration on it, and once it actually ticked....   The hut was also decorated with old metal advertising plaques, nowadays fashionable as ornaments.   These, too, have ben removed, possibly sold to some nostalgia-hungry American oilman.   There is a wooden floor for comfort, and the uneven walls have many places on which to place candles, which create a magical flicker and glow.

One advantage of the howff is its size.   Though too low to stand up in, it is easy to heat in the coldest weather, by the expedient of keeping a couple of primuses burning.   Bliss it was to warm up in the hiss of the primuses after a day on the hill, and sit in the light of the flickering candles deciphering the runic inscriptions on the walls.   *Fish Pies* repeated over and over induced a nirvana-like state of bliss, and was always a favourite, though *Tot Heid* was a rival.   Who had scrawled

The Howff

them, and in what state of mind? Erase them not, some day they may offer an archeologist clues to bothy life.

Because of the location, Slugain Howff can be a dangerous place to head for in bad weather, even for those who have frequented it. On one occasion, Stumpy and a pal descended from the bus at the Invercauld gates, and made their way up the glen, along a snow-covered path, with the sky full of more snow. This soon began to fall quickly, and the path gradually disappeared. Progress was slow through deep drifts of soft snow, and they knew the howff was not easy to find, even in clear summer weather. But with the path obscured, spindrift swirling and legs tiring, the difficulties were increased, and thoughts of retreat, or an emergency bivouac at Slugain ruins, were entertained. Seemingly endless distances were covered, and a mild panic ensued, since they would soon be on the open moor with no shelter at all. But gradually this passed, and Stumpy's pal began to feel that this would be a marvellous way to expire, amid all this soft white beauty. Luckily, the outline of the tell-tale marker that indicates the way to the howff was soon discerned through the blur of snow. As usual, relief led to a sudden access of energy, and the duo scrambled to the top of the outcrop.

As the second man arrived at the top, he was greeted with the groans and curses of his companion, a man normally of so few words that something clearly was amiss. 'It's gone, the bugger's gone,' Stumpy gabbled incoherently. 'The howff, it's gone.'

And horror was added to horror when his ice axe pointed at a smooth expanse of snow, sloping ahead of them. Stupefaction was the initial reaction, but soon numbed brains realised that the howff was buried in the drift. They attacked the snow with ice axes, roughly where they felt the door must be. Labours ended when a way to the door was cleared. Inside the door lay a spade for just such contingencies, and the man who left it there must have heard the curses, as the companions collapsed inside the howff, as its proper place was outside the dor.

They slunk into sleeping bags and slept, but on wakening, found that fresh snow falls had again blocked the entrance, and they had to dig themselves out.   Waist high snow confined them to the bothy that weekend, but buried in snow, the howff acted like an igloo.   While sub-zero temperatures ruled outside, they sat stripped to their shirts, with the stoves roaring.

Normally the object of a trip to the howff was of course Beinn a Bhuird.   The usual route was to follow the path up the Quoich to the Sneck between our mountain and Ben Avon, passing *en route* the huge Clach a Chleirich boulder, marked on the map as a ruin, but it was never a building.   From there the route passes the lip of the vast Garbh Choire, giving easy access to the north summit.   The summit of Beinn a Bhuird, like much of the Cairngorms, is a semi-desert, almost devoid of vegetation, yet nevertheless still abounding in ptarmigan and dotterel.   From this summit the route skirting the high corries is an easy one, and leads to the south top, and thence down the shoulder of Corrie na Ciche to the edges of the Quoich pine woods, and back to Slugain.

The views on this route down Glen Quoich are particularly fine, with its landscape of river and Scots pine.   This is an alternative route to Braemar, and though rough and trackless at first, it gradually improves, but involves a by no means unhazardous crossing of the Dee by fording.   It passes the Punch Bowl, a pool in the river where the Earl of Mar is supposed to have brewed a huge punch to launch the 1715 Jacobite rebellion.

Another route to the summit of Beiunn a Bhuird is to enter one of the high corries, and ascend by any of the easy screes, such as the Main Rake.   As an alternative day out from the howff, there was Ben Avon.   This is not a very interesting ascent, but is amply repaid by examining and scrambling over the many weird and wonderful tors which adorn its vast summit plateau.   Dartmoor, thy pleasures are pale and domestic, compared with these.   And from the summit of Ben Avon, a truly epic sweep of the four corries of Beinn a Bhuird opens out to the wondering eye.

A more adventurous trip was to to leave the howff at Slugain after the first night, laboriously re-pack rucksacks and head off for a stay in the 'high Howff' in the corrie, one of the greatest delights known to man or beast. Some of the earliest climbers on Beinn a Bhuird, in order to maximise their period of proximity to the rock faces, gave the artefacts of nature a helping hand. Selecting large boulders perched on their sisters, they built up protective walls round gaps, and constructed primitive shelters that would protect body and soul in all but extreme conditions.

The best in the Beinn a Bhuird area is under the second largest boulder in Corrie nan Clach (appropriately, *Corrie of the Stones)*. Named after two of the pioneers, the Smith/Winram howff is no secret, being mentioned in the original Cairngorm S.M.C. guide. But its remoteness means that it is seldom used, compared to its Lochnagar rival, for example. But for those willing to undergo extreme discomfort, nothing can compare with waking on a glorious morning, to summer sun or winter snow, in the high corries, with the light already on the cliffs behind — unless it be having the sublime luck to spend a starlit evening seated at a high doss, your troubles as far away as the heavens themselves.

However, even the most sublime settings can have their ridiculous accompaniments. Three men, accompanied by an intrepid mutt, had gained their destination one evening, after a long, unbroken walk from Invercauld — something of a feat with full packs. The high doss took three at a push, and his pals had argued, with statistical evidence, that the cubic space was insufficent to accommodate the brute as well. However, like most canine owners, he was convinced that proximity to his beloved best friend would make the hearts of the other two grow fonder towards it, and he brushed their objections aside. After a hurried meal, the company began to arrange themselves as pleasantly as possible in a space little more than seven feet long, by five wide and three feet high, rucksacks blocking the door against wind and weather.

But doubtless upset by his strange surroundings, the hound refused to settle, and trampled restlessly, whining, over the recumbent figures. Mutterings of hostility were accompanied by renewed reference to previous mathamatical computations of howff space, and the owner of the beast began to fear its eviction. Thinking that it might be cold, it was forced into the foot of a sleeping bag, where it presently slept. In the morning, as bodies began to move, a mollified voice asked, 'Foo's the dog?'

His drowsy owner prodded him with a foot, which produced no response. Confusion and fright mingled in his sleepy head.

"He's nae moving: he must be deid,' he cried, and leaped up, promptly reeling back semi-conscious, as his head cracked into the boulder overhead. At this point the mutt stirred, scrambled out of the bag, and frisked off to cock his leg in the corrie. Though they said nothing, his companions were clearly convinced that poetic justice had been done, and were remarkably friendly to the brute for the rest of the day. Since then its owner has got into the habit of sleeping with a bunnet on to avoid collisions in high dosses — and he leaves all quadrupeds at home.

Though Slugain howff was one of the homes-from-home of the newer generation of north-east climbers in the late 1960s and early 70s, such characters did not claim all the proprietorial rights one might have expected. Slugain was never exclusive, unlike its counterpart Jacksonville. An Aberdonian offended by the company is more likely to vote with his feet than respond with his fists. The attitude was that if you found it, or were introduced to it, you could use it. An anecdote may illustrate this.

On one occasion, a young mountaineer occupied Slugain in the company of a young lady who was kidding on she loved the outdoor life, and a dog (already known to the reader),who really did. A pleasant weekend of strolls and amorous pursuits *al fresco* was envisaged. Both plans were to be disturbed by the entry of two great men, famed in guide books but who shall be nameless. After the usual exchange of pleasantries, one of the *illuminati* asked what the mountaineer intended to do 'the morn'. Despite the fact that his companion was of the then fashionable liberated persuasion, he was still at an age when the defense of his masculinity in front of the fair sex was of some importance. He replied, with a resigned sigh towards his female and canine accompaniments, 'Well, nae much. Possibly a bit of solo scrambling.'

'Try Slab and Arrete; it's only moderate, wi' a diff. pitch,' came the friendly advice.

Next day, while the real things headed off towards Garbh Coire, the fake article was in a quandary. Moderate or not, he had never soloed anything steeper than a flight of stairs in his life. On return to the bothy at night he could of course lie, but what would the damsel think? There was nothing else for it, so the trio headed for the climb, which divides the corries of nan Clach and Dubh Lochan. At the base the route up the Main Rake was outlined to the admiring lovely, who was left with the dog, as her hero began the ascent. He scrambled easily enough up the easy-angled slabs to the foot of the arrete. Hysterical barking now disturbed him as he contemplated the next stage. Once out of sight, the young lady had let the dog off his lead — a fatal mistake. It darted to the base of the slabs, and at breakneck speed darted up them, to compete for space with its beloved master at the foot of the arrete, its tail wagging in delight.

Astonished as he was at the animal's climbing ability, its owner realised that the arrete was beyond its powers. After some thought, it was bundled into his rucksack, which was slung back on. The beast wriggled about on his back as he moved up the arrete, until its head emerged from under his left armpit to lick his face. In canine bliss and masculine trepidation they moved up the final chimney to the summit plateau. They arrived back in the howff earlier than the real men, who had sported with a few V. Diffs. on the Garbh Choire.

'Why are they V. Diff. and you're only Moderate?' queried the damsel.

'But I made history the day!'

'How?'

'First ascent Slab and Arrete, man and dog!'

Occasionally, however, conflicts did occur. On one occasion a party of regular users arrived to find the door jammed closed by some heavy impediment. Their attempts to push it open were greeted with a shout of 'There's nae room in here.'

The siege party was in a quandary; there was no telling the strength of the possessing party, should events turn nasty. There was no alternative place to doss, so forcing an entry was imperative. The first step was to demand entry, and this was accompanied by battering on the corrugated iron roof. The reply was to invite the besiegers to remove themselves to some place, but there was a hint of a less confident tone to the utterance, which gave the newcomers courage. The door was eventually pushed back, but jammed against what turned out to be an interior palisade of sacks and other gear. There was only one alternative to an undignified and exposed scramble over these.

'There's plenty of space here', muttered the assault leader, as he humped the sacks, and projected them outside, 'Plenty of room.' The occupants, encased in sleeping bags, were at a distinct strategic disadvantage, and watched in amazement as their gear vanished into the void.

But never did they stir, nor hardly spoke, and the assault party began to feel a little embarrassed at their blitzkrieg tactics, as the defenders were revealed as little more than puppies, and fewer in number than the attackers. Peering from their sleeping bags, they watched as possession passed to another party, occupying their *lebensraum* by right of conquest, and busily brewing up. Gradually a thaw set in, and the lads' gear was fetched and handed to them. Once the tea had 'masked' they were offered some.

'We were feart: that's why we blocked the door.'

The presence of such an uninitiated audience encouraged the telling of tales of other entries, and of nights in the open. It was not only to boast, but also to convey to the youngsters a realisation that the need of others for shelter far outweighs the desire for solitude, or claims of propriety by earlier occupants of a howff, and that this was the elementary maxim of bothy ethics.

One tale told that night deserves retelling here, if only because it concerns a location in the environs of Ben Avon. Its hero was Mealy Pudding, a man whose adopted name conveyed his capacities as an omnivore. As well as being a gargantuan eater (a double fish supper was only *hors d'oevre* for him), Mealy was a hypochondriac, a walking dispensary with pills for every ailment his mind could imagine. If you needed to move your bowels, Mealy had the wherewithal, likewise if you needed to stop them moving. Headaches, stomach pains, insomnia, Old Doc Pudding could provide something for them all. Mealy was always complaining about his aches and pains, with the result you could never get him on a hill without him fainting or doubling up with cramp. He was also a laugh a minute; if he uttered more than a monosyllabic grunt every half hour, you'd be overwhelmed at his garrulousness.

Mealy was a youth always desirous of change. All trips went up Deeside, but Mealy suggested one up Donside, to gain Ben Avon's northern flanks. There were two problems. The bus stopped at Strathdon. He offered his motorbike as the solution to the last 15 miles after he'd met his partner off the bus. The second problem was that there was nowhere to stay.

'There's the boat house at Loch Builg', was the confident reply.

Those words were the overture to near disaster. The first part of the trip, along the douce Don, was idyllic. This was followed by an exhilarating bike ride, with his partner dismounting at the steep bits, along to Inchrory Lodge. Then, packs on backs, they advanced south to the Boat House. There it was, thankfully, with its roof intact. But on approach, it was revealed that its walls were not. In fact, they gave access to at least three of the four winds. And those seemed to be the three that were blowing that day. As night fell, the temperature began to plummet.

The night was a nightmare. It was impossible to sleep, and the duo periodically spent time hopping about in their sleeping bags to keep circulation going.

'Great training for a sack race', muttered Mealy's partner, and Mealy began to think that the weekend might not be a success after all. How cold it was that night is impossible to say, but in the morning the loch was frozen over. It was so cold that the stoves would not light; the paraffin refusing to vaporise. Without breakfast, they abandoned camp and fled for the motor bike. Since then, whenever the lack of bothies in the vicinity of Ben Avon has been mentioned, the unsuspecting have been informed: 'There's always the boat house at Loch Builg!'

The exits for the adventurous from Slugain howff are quite varied. Apart from a simple retreat down Glen Slugain, or the alternative by the Quoich already mentioned, there is the possibility of crossing the mountain to Faindouran Lodge in Glen Avon, where there is an open bothy maintained by the M.B.A. After the troglodyte existence of Slugain, Faindouran is luxury indeed, with furniture and fire. It is an old shooting lodge, no longer used by today's day-tripper sportsmen, who at Inchrory have every conceivable comfort. The bothy is the end apartment, and like the Lodge has suffered from vandals, being at one time reputedly the home of a semi-hermit who cannibalised it. Humble talks of Faindouran in former days as 'the bothy with the best fireplace in the Cairngorms' (Scots Magazine, Nov. 1969), though the area round it is conspicuous for its lack of fuel of any kind. From Faindouran you can go downriver to Inchrory, and out to a road at Corgarff, or head upstream to the fords of Avon, and thence northwards to Ryvoan bothy and Rothiemurchus.

A final possibility is to exit to the west, by crossing Beinn a Bhuird and descending to the high moss of Moine Bhealaid, and thence to Glen Derry and either the Etchachan hut, or the welcoming woods of Derry and Luibeg. Though this exit shows you our mountain's disappointing western flank, it allows for a marvellous view of Coire Etchachan and Ben Macdui. On a good day, the springy moss can provide a carpet underfoot for walking past high lochans which tempt the walker for a bathe in the water, followed by one in the sun, watching the deer and listening to the black cock.

There are many things men promise themselves to repeat, but never do. This is possibly to protect nostalgia from the hammer blows of reality, to cherish an illusion rather than face disappointment. But after many years, it was still a delight to bow down and enter again that dwarf's door leading to the Secret Howff. It was pleasing to see that the howff was still being repaired, with new floor and gutters. The hut book showed that the frequency of use was still low, indicating that the secret is still being handed on by word of mouth. One hut book has served for almost 20 years. Many of the same names keep cropping up, including those of former comrades whose capacity to invent excuses for not climbing shows no sign of declining. The inanities of the casual visitor are missing from this log book, which deserved to be preserved. There was one familiar entry, and perhaps that carefully penned entry, complete with Kipling quote will excuse the company he was in. A couple of west coasters had accompanied him there, but at least they did admit that the howff was a unique gem, with no rival in Scotland (and that the Cumming Crofton route wasn't *too* bad). It is a precious thing to have experienced the magic of this Arcanium, which has become a part of Scottish mountain history, nay, mythology. Long may it remain as it is, the last of the bothies to be maintained unofficially, and known to its users only by oral tradition.

The Fire

BEN NEVIS

At certain times in the history of mountaineering, some places become the target of frenzied activity and development. They become the 'in' place to climb. Personal knowledge of their routes, names dropped, sometimes quietly, though more often boastfully, into the conversation in the pub, are the mark of the tiger — the man who is at the forefront of things.

Ben Nevis in the winter is one place that seems to have sustained this kind of reputation for longer than most. At one time, if there were half a dozen parties on the mighty north face this was considered busy. Nowadays it is like Sauchiehall Street on a Saturday afternoon. And it is not only the Scots and the English who swell the crowds, for it is possible to share a cold belay with men who have turned their backs on their native and more glamorous Rockies or Alps.

There is no doubt about the main cause of all this feverish activity. It is the revolutionary new tools introduced in the late sixties that turned iceclimbing in Scotland from an esoteric, sado-masochistic sport indulged in by a few over-muscled, mad Scots, into something everybody and his mum could do, and even enjoy. The reader may feel this to be a disparaging over-exaggeration. However, at the time of the introduction of ice axes with the new curved picks, this writer distinctly remembers being told by a leading member of a famous Edinburgh-based mountaineering club that they made winter climbing 'too easy', and therefore ought to be banned.

The greater numbers of climbers have, of course, brought with them conmensurately greater problems. Of these, the increased number of deaths is the most serious, and despite the fact that many English mountaineers are superb climbers, some do over-extend themselves or else seem poorly prepared for the long distances, low temperatures and ravages of wind that often await them. Hence they are over-represented in the casualty lists. So much so that there is a black, black joke that falls from the lips of the more chauvinistic of the Scottish climbing fraternity. Scottish winter climbing, they say, is Scotland's revenge for Culloden.

There is another associated but less dramatic problem that so far has not attracted much publicity. Students of Scottish mountaineering literature will no doubt recall W.H. Murray's enthusiastic description of the 'gay colours of the mountain' in his account of a winter ascent of Observatory Ridge on the Ben's north face. Today's visitor can add another colour to Murray's inventory of *ebony towers...pale brown ridges....cream of a cornice.....sheen of green ice....silver icicles......* , for, if he wanders to the north-east of the Charles Inglis Clarke Memorial Hut, he will find, near a large boulder, the golden glacier. It is without doubt the most disgusting sight to be seen in the Scottish mountains — the frozen, semi-frozen and fresh collection of human ordure left behind by men whose bowels, as well as spirits, have been moved by the sight of the mighty north face.

This glacial cesspool is the most explicit sign of pressure on the famous C.I.C. Hut, for it must be, in the winter months anyway, one of the most sought-after pieces of real estate in the world of British mountaineering. Standing on its spur of ancient morraine below the huge complications that comprise the Ben's north face, with its thick wall and heavily shuttered windows, it resembles a small fort. Obviously its architecture is largely determined by the fearsome inclemencies of weather experienced at those altitudes. Jerry-build here, and there would be little in the way of a home to come home to. However, it is also suspected that the ruggedness of the building is designed to deter break-ins by unregistered guests.   Hence the bars over the windows.

Such precautions, unfortunately, seem to be justified, for over the years the C.I.C. Hut has received more than its fair share of attention from those determined not to pay for their night's accommodation.   In the sixties, however, to achieve illegal entry did not require violence to be done to the building, for there was a loose bar which could be removed to allow access to the window.   How the bar became loose is anybody's guess, and most explanations centre around deterioration of the fabric caused by the weather.   Others were less naive, and rumour had it that the wilder, younger element of a certain mountaineering club were responsible for this nicety of unspecified design.

Of course, if the hut was already occupied, break-ins were not necesary.   In that case, the technique of 'brassnecking' was used. This inevitably led to conflicts such as the one some Glasgow itinerants had with a gentleman of the older, more conservative element from Edinburgh.   The former had arrived through a fiercely gathering storm, late on a Saturday afternoon.   They had installed themselves and were busy trying to see how far up the steel lum of the old pot-bellied stove they could force the red hot mark, when they were made aware by others in the hut that there was a party still abroad in what was now a very foul night.   The wind was crashing against the thick walls making the hut shudder.   Outside, the snow came down in blankets.

Six o'clock, seven, eight and still no sign of them.   Everybody in the hut became subdued as each one privately considered the implications of the non-appearance.   It would be their duty to put on some kind of search, even though under the conditions it would be no more than tokenism.   As nine o'clock approached the depth of anxiety of the occupants was manifested by their silence.   The usually exuberant Glaswegians were significantly quiet.   They were more than a bit concerned about that missing group.

Finally, as patience and optimism were ebbing low, the outside door was opened and the noise of stamping boots was heard above the aggressively ransacking wind. Everybody inside relaxed, stretched and smiled. They were back, thank God they were safe, no need for them to venture out. However, this calmness was shortlived, for through the inner door came this tall figure encased in snow. He ignored the welcoming words, obviously oblivious to the concern he and his group had engendered, and asked crossly of the 'brassneckers': 'Are you booked?' No mug this one: he spotted them immediately.

Taken aback by the hostility from one who only minutes earlier was the object of altruistic concern and proposed searches in dangerous conditions, the attitude of the Glasgow lads hardened. Their answer 'No, what's it to you?' set the tone for the rest of the evening. The Glasgow boys, although they regained their composure and to some extent their humour, sat around the stove more subdued than usual, while in the corner, the latecomer surrounded himself with his chums and muttered dark things about people who used the hut but did not pay.

With hindsight it is difficult to defend the delinquent attitudes of the Glaswegians. After all, the C.I.C. Hut was not an open bothy, but a club hut with superb facilities that were expensive to maintain and ought to have been paid for. On the other hand, however, solid sons of the horny-handed proletariat that they were, the boys were perhaps inadvertently creating the kind of society envisaged for them by their philosopher king, Karl Marx, when he wrote *From each according to his ability, to each according to his need.*

All this matters little now. The C.I.C. Hut is so well defended by steel shutters and locks on the locks that Johnny Ramenski could not break in. Moreover, judging from recent stories from this high place, the S.M.C. inmates seem to be short-necked, short-tempered individuals whose attitudes to interlopers are akin to those held by bouncers at a Glasgow dance hall. No-one steps over their tightly drawn lines of decorum. 'Brassnecking' is now a dangerous pastime.

It has already been said that winter climbing on the Ben is also a dangerous pastime. Here the newcomer has a problem. To cope with the dangers he must get experience, yet in gaining that experience he is at his most vulnerable. Of course, there is plenty of expert advice available. But how much of it is practical? It seems a little bit complacent of some experts to write about the infectious fever of climbing that drives men crazy for adventure on the mountain, yet at the same time asks them to exercise extreme caution in learning the craft. Caution obviously there must be, but it is not every youngster who wants to join a club, or has the money for courses at Glenmore Lodge. The most common solution used to be the apprenticeship. Young lads would climb with the more experienced, and in return they were expected to do the dreary domestic tasks round the bothy — fetch the water, peel the tatties, that sort of thing. They used to have a very racist piece of terminology to describe such a lad — a blackboy. Later, and in an informal way the young, now more experienced, would drift off on their own, form new groups, acquire their own apprentices. But even this system had its flaws.

Some beginners, like the two wee boys from Possil once spotted on the Cobbler in their sanies trying to climb Right Angle Gully Direct with their maw's clothes rope, do not know any experts. Moreover, even when contact is made, there are difficulties, for the aspirants' arrangements cannot always coincide with those of their masters. To gain experience they must get out and climb, and climbing without experience means that they must, in ignorance, break the rules. Rule breaking can be minimised, but most, if they are honest, will admit that they have indulged in it. Many will deny it, mistaking survival for competence. But it cannot be denied: it is fate which, in the early years, divides the victims from the survivors.

Ignorant they certainly were, those two seventeen year olds, who wandered out of the C.I.C. Hut into the indifferent weather of a late Sunday morning. It was mildish and the cloud level was well down. But the weather was not the only thing that was indifferent that day. Those two had very little idea of what they were about. For a start, they had no real target in mind. They had heard that Tower Ridge was a good classic climb, and not too hard. Some-one in the hut had pointed it out to them, so they wandered up there to

143

have a look.   Secondly, they were not very well equipped: a hundred feet of laid nylon rope, big, long ice-axes and a few slings and caribiners was their lot.   True, they had crampons, but they were ex-army ones, designed for use with overboots, and as a consequence, next to useless.   They had no guidebook and no knowledge of the route, although they did have a map and compass and a hand torch.

It was late, around one in the afternoon, when they poked their noses into the wee gully behind the Douglas Boulder.   It did not look so bad, so, despite some misgivings about the late hour, the brave boys were encouraged to climb the steep step onto the ridge proper.   Any apprehension they had soon disappeared when they found they were travelling on relatively easy ground that consisted of narrow ridges of kickable snow, pitched at a shallow angle.   Perhaps, argued one, they ought to move together for speed.   He had been reading books about the Alps and had been impressed by the authors' claims that speed sometimes contributed more to safety than did careful belaying. His companion, however, lacked his literary turn of mind, and, eyeing the steep drops on both sides of their slender walkway, argued most strongly for the painfully slow, but safe, anchoring of the rope at each pitch.   In his ignorance, how was he to know he still had 1800 feet to go, with all the major difficulties above?

In this way ignorance spins a web into which the naive are easily drawn.   The optimism of their casual, unfounded belief in themselves was reinforced by the relative ease of their passage.   They were now in thick cloud, but the only difficulties so far encountered were some little rocky steps devoid of snow and ice.   So up they went, quite pleased with themselves.   Real climbers, we are, they thought.   How far is it to the top?

And then, on what was the first serious steepening, the atmosphere changed from uninformed relaxation to uninformed anxiety.   Here the rock, though slabby, had a number of awkward-looking steps on it.   It was also much higher than its predecessors and, although the mist did not permit much in the way of vision, the ground on the left, where the way seemed to lie, disappeared into a luminous, silver-grey abyss. Apart from this, the rock of what they were later to find was called 'The Little Tower' appeared to be clear of anything frozen, just like those below.

The first confident step up showed this to be an illlusion. Rubbing his scraped knee, the leader, who had just rattled off the lower slab to collapse in a heap in the snow below, told his companion that the rock was covered with a thin, clear layer of ice. Lacking the knowledge that this impediment to their progress was called verglas did not stop the leader fabricating a technique to deal with the problem. For this, his long and unwieldly ice-axe came into play, for despite the fact that its use upset his balance, he used it to roughen up the ice to allow some purchase for the commando soles of his bendy boots.

In that manner he proceeded to the top of the outcrop without apparent difficulty. Success like this, so easily gained, quickens the heart and emboldens the spirit. So on went the two adventurers through the grey light of the mountain fog, on to the unseen and unknown difficulties and terrors.

The first of these was a huge gloomy steepness that reared out of the mist like the prow of some great stranded ship. Its frost-encrusted flanks looked impossible. A conumdrum of secret smoothness within which, argued the intellects below, must lie the solution, for others have passed this way. To find it, first one, then the other tried to force a way up the hoary rock. There was no solution to be had among the gasping, cursing thrashings. Much chastened and more than a little worried, for the grey light was beginning to turn a little bit darker, the two looked first to the right, and then to the left of the bulwark. While the right flank looked dire, the left offered hope in the shape of an airy, traversing weakness.

One set off, cutting steps leftwards on the now perfect snow. Awkward at first, round a bulge, but then no more difficulties until an uncomfortable icy step-up had to be made. Though the poor light and thick mist prevented him from seeing it, he sensed the exposure. Ice pieces slithered downwards, the muffled sound of their descent indicating the depth they fell. Tired legs trembled a bit in the scurry upwards. Then on again, arms tired by the labour of cutting, until the ice encrusted rock above suggested access to the ridge. Belay here and let the other solve this problem.

This he did with knees on the rock, feet flailing and much heavy breathing. To hell with style! In winter anything goes — the head, teeth, anything! Just get up before it gets dark. Above, the rock gave onto easier ground which in turn led to a knife-edge ridge of snow. He shuffled crab-like along this, careful to keep his balance in the wind he suddenly realised was rising. Had it been there before unnoticed in the concentration of the struggle, or had it sprung up with malevolent intent from the unseen void? The questions flitted through his mind, but he thought of no answer, for he was looking at something that made his heart sink.

He had now reached a widening in the ridge where he could stand comfortably alongside what must have been a huge boulder encrusted with snow. Beyond that was a huge hole in the ridge. A gap, maybe eight feet wide with a ten feet drop. *'Jeeeeesus!'* he breathed to himself as he prepared to bring up his pal.

The reaction was terse. 'How the fuck do ye get across that?' Unfortunately, his language sometimes deteriorated in moments of stress. 'Maybe ye jump it?' suggested the other. The lack of confidence in his voice betrayed his lack of confidence in this method. 'Don't be daft; look at yon big pillar on the other side. Ye'd have to have a rocket up yer arse to get on top of that.' Stress once again played havoc with his language. 'Aye, right enough,' assented the other, 'but we'll have to get a move on. It's getting dark.'

In the end, they did the right thing. In the fast-gathering dusk one was lowered by the other into the gap. From there, he climbed the pillar on the other side. His feet slipped at times and ice particles rattled off down a horrible looking chimney on his right. A couple of times his body also looked inclined to rattle off down the same chimney, but in the end, and now in total darkness, he got up. Much relieved, he pushed on upwards.

146

His companion sat in a stupor, his mind freezing in the numbing wind. The rope, his guarantee of safety over the hidden terror, slipped slowly through his hands. He was not happy. This was one of the rare occasions when the second man, at least for the first part of the pitch, was more at risk than the leader. He would have to untie the rope and abseil into the gap. Not a prospect he relished in the darkness and wind. After a while the rope stopped moving. Shortly came a voice made weak by the strength of the wind. The words chilled his already frozen heart. 'Don't fa aff: there's nae belay.'

When he arrived in the gap it was black. So black, he had no sensation of anything except the incipient anxiety of his stomach that was trying to invade his chest in wild panic. At the time, the source of his fear was not something about which he thought. However, in retrospect, it has become clearer. There were no terms of reference. He felt as if he were floating in a featureless black void. His unseen feet were mere appendages, not of his body, but of his imagination. At that moment they felt as though they were placed, none too firmly, on uneven rock and ice. Movement opened up possibilities of falling.

Then there was the wind. Bad enough by now on the ridge above, but, forced through the gap, it felt worse, much worse. It tugged and pushed at him, demanding movement, a stagger, a lurch into the void. This, he thought, is what it is like to die.

In the darkness, cool thought fled in panic. The terror whispered to him — why not end it now? Extinguish the horrendous anxiety with a leap into the void. It soaked his brain like some negative adrenalin. End It! Go on, jump! Vertigo, yet he could not see anything except blackness and more blackness.

But no, the life force was still there. That part of the mind that fears the fall instructs the fingers to sort out the wind-tangled mess of rope, and, eventually, miraculously, he is tied on again. His brain became clearer. Thoughts of the possibilities of survival returned. He turned to where he thought the pillar was, and began his attempt at climbing it. Later, friends would ask him: how did you get up? He could not see the holds for hand or foot, and he dare not ask for aid from the rope, for he could have dislodged his companion from his stance. The truth is that he does not know. All he can remember were desperate, slow movements in the black void that somehow provided adhesion. He was lucky: he made it. That is all.

The ground was easier now, but still the climb was not at an end. The mountain still had one last surprise for them. This time, a pleasant one, for suddenly the mist lifted, and just for a brief moment the strange magnificence of their situation was revealed to them. They were just beneath the summit plateau, and by a freakish, opaque moonlight, filtered through thin mist, they glimpsed an amphitheatre of wonderful complexity. Huge double cornices, ice and snow pillars of awesome proportions and terrifying steepness were all around. A white, but uncompleted, natural cathedral that compelled them to stop and gaze despite the lateness of the hour. It was so utterly alien that it did not look like a place for men, yet there they were. Still there — so far. Then it went black again as if the light had been switched off by an unseen hand. It had been, for them, a unique experience, for they were never to see such a phenomenom again in twenty years of climbing.

After that, the plateau was an anti-climax It often is, even after the completion of a hard climb to which one has looked forward, and prepared for over many months or even years. Let others talk enthusiastically and noisily about the joys of 'conquering' mountains; wiser men take a quieter pleasure in the satisfaction of a more realistic notion. They have come to terms with the mountain, survived on its alien slopes, have learned to live with it. And while they are now more familiar with a sliver of geography, they have learned much more about themselves. In this case they had been frightened by the difficulties created by their own inexperience, but they had survived. They were lucky, and they knew it.

Still they had to get down through the blackness and mist. One had a compass and the theoretical knowledge of how to use. Here practice would have made perfection, for into his mind seeped the stories he had heard of innocents who strayed over the huge northern cliffs, or who, in their determination to avoid them, slipped disastrously into the web of gullies on the Glen Nevis side of the mountain. They had heard that there was an easy gully that would take them directly to the hut, but they agreed that under the present circumstances they would be very unlikely to find it. They would have to make for the Red Burn and walk round the bottom of the cliffs to the hut. A long way, but a safe one. Just the same, they know now that the descent of the Red Burn should not be underestimated, for just after this was written came the sad news that two men had died there after being caught in an avalanche.

In later years the two have returned, though not always together, and other ascents of the ridge have been done by them. Sometimes it was done in summer with lasses from Glenmore Lodge who wept at the sight of the gap, and sometimes in winter via the excellent Italian Climb. The luck of that first ascent has never been forgotten. Once, when setting out for a winter's day on the ridge from the Hut, one of those young lads and his companion were hailed by a young man whose breathing and face betrayed his anxiety. He gasped out his story. He and his friend had been avalanched under the Garadh Gully, and while he had got out, he could not find his friend.

His friend was unlucky. They dug him out without a mark on him, but he was quite, quite dead. As he listened to the insensitivity of some stupid mountain rescue team leader (not from the local Lochaber team) who had decided to use the body as a visual aid for a smug little lecture on the dangers of avalanches, he could not help feeling angry, sad and fatalistic. More experienced now, he would not have said that the hill was particularly avalanche prone that day, yet the young man who lay at his feet, manifestly better equipped than he and his companion of earlier days, and probably not half as ignorant, was dead. He had broken some barely perceptible rule of nature, and he paid the ultimate price. They had broken a thousand rules, yet had lived to become more experienced, more cautious, mortgaged and superannuated. Fate separates the survivors from the victims.

Bob Scott's

BOB SCOTT'S

There are bothies which change their character, but few which change their names. Any one may decline through misuse or the ravages of weather, or improve due to the efforts of a dedicated work-party. Any rise or decline in popularity affects the general character of a doss, via the residue of human artifacts. But what the map shows as Luibeg, and what the present generation refers to in that way, to their predecessors was always rather 'Bob Scott's' – and the passing of the years have altered it in more than name. Sadly, the final passing of Scott's must now be marked, for recently it was burned to the ground.

Scott's lay about 10 miles from Braemar, just before the Luibeg (Little Lui) burn runs into the Derry burn at Derry Lodge. Luibeg cottage is on on the south side of the burn, its back turned towards the massif of Macdui. Formerly, the cottage was in full-time occupation by a gamekeeper, Bob Scott, and his daughter, and had been for as long as anyone could remember. The actual bothy, a timber outhouse, stood near the cottage. Often it was a Friday night target. Leaving the bus at Braemar, the party would trudge the metalled misery of the road to Mar Lodge, and after a couple of fortifying pints, battle over the 'back road' to the Black Bridge and thence up Glen Lui to Luibeg.

There were reasons other than the convivial for stopping at Mar. There was the almost inevitable failure to cadge a lift from Braemar, but during the time spent there waiting in hope, some would tell of the halycon days when Mar ran a free bus from Braemar to their Friday dances, and climbers masqueraded as customers before slipping off to Scott's, to which others would reply nostalgically with tales of the old Strachans' buses which plied the south Deeside road, without timetables and, it was suspected, without brakes. Hope would rise eternal that 'Scott would be in the bar at Mar Lodge.' The logic behind this was as follows: if Scott was there, and in a good mood, and if you bought him drink, you could ride the last four miles or so to Luibeg in his Land Rover. Looking back, the prospect of a ride over a rough road, on a dark night with a driver who was far from teetotal, in a truck full of guns and dogs, does not seem too attractive, but it did at the time. Not that such luck ever befell anyone you knew or met, but some told of others who had told them that it had happened to yet others, and this served as an encouragement.

Sometimes Scott did condescend to notice aspiring lift-fodder, and let himself be bought some liquid sustenance. On one occasion, as closing-time passed, and Scott showed no sign of moving, those who had courted him were rewarded with: 'You loons had better awa tae Derry. It's a lang wye on a dark nicht.' They slunk out into the cold, and later heard their host arriving some time in the wee sma' hours, doubtless chuckling to hmself.

On another occasion, two hopefuls had been supplying the usual libations, when Scott went out, ostensibly to relieve nature. But the last they heard of him that night was the roar of his vehicle as it sped away without them. Clearly, the man believed that mountaineers should stand on their own feet. In the bar, disappointment led to further alcoholic indulgence, and when the two emerged from the pub at 10 o'clock, they were in no physical or spiritual state for the next four miles, and began looking for somewhere to doss down. There was an open hut, built of old bucolic junk nearby. It was also full of a soft, snowy-white substance, that the lads, in their euphoria, took to be cotton wool. Rejoicing in their luck, they bedded down. Morning revealed that one of them had been so drunk he had pulled his sleeping bag out of his rucksack, and then climbed into the rucksack to sleep. It also revealed that the 'cotton wool' was artificial snow, whose fibres covered hands and faces with blisters, and impregnated sleeping bags. It was a miserable party that headed for the pub at opening time again, before eventually reaching Luibeg late in the afternoon.

Though he revelled in his status as a worthy, and latterly became something of a media celebrity, even achieving the ultimate accolade of a picture in the most recent SMC Cairngorm guide beside that of Patey, Scott clearly regarded himself as a gamekeeper, rather than some decorative attendant to mountaineers. He did not court attention, and only occasionally talked to bothy occupants. The favoured few might well remember the experience. On one occasion a mountaineer was preparing for the day ahead, when Scott entered the bothy.

'Div ye want tae see me feeding my kye?', he asked.

He was a man to humour, and the mountaineer agreed, musing at this increase in Scott's agricultural functions. Chickens were to be seen running about the cottage, but *cattle?*. Outside Scott held a bucket of cattle cake aloft, and grinning, banged it with his spade. Out of the Derry woods came dozen after dozen of red deer, and crossed the river towards Scott. Their coats were worn and their bodies lean with hunger after the hard winter. He fed them virtually by hand, and they would go near no other person, though he would be the main agent of their later death. He brought the interview to an end with: 'It's yokin' time. Ye'd better awa up yer hill.'

Scott ran the bothy on fairly *laissez-faire* lines, though there were certain rules that were rigorously enforced. He imposed an impost on all overnight travellers, which he rigorously extracted. Tales were told of him pursuing defaulting fugitives up Glen Derry in his Land Rover. It was one shilling from time immemorial, but when decimalisation was introduced, Scott took the opportunity to increase it to 10p. 'That's only ten pence', he would say, as if in fact the charge had been reduced. And he forbade anyone to use the rotting abandoned fence posts around Luibeg for fuel, and insisted that you scoured the Derry woods, where in fact it was plentiful. Desperate Dan had a rare fire going one day when in burst Scott, and hauled the fence posts blazing from the fire, to loose an outburst of colourful invective on the startled occupant.

At Luibeg a light was always left burning in the back window of the cottage, for the aid of anyone benighted in the hills. Feet used to quicken when you saw its flicker through the Derry woods, but no more does it greet the traveller. Bob Scott retired in the early 1970s, and left Luibeg for the Quoich, where he lived in retirement. The cottage at Luibeg, a victim of estate rationalisation, is vacant much of the year now, and only used occasionally by the new gamekeeper. The bothy, however, remained open to all comers, but alas no longer had the electric light, powered by an oil generator, for which the overnight tax was imposed. A cobweb covered bulb remained as the only symbolical reminder of the 'bothy with electricity'. After Scott left, the bothy was free, but without Scott, a character the like of which one meets too seldom, Luibeg and the whole of the Cairngorms are much the poorer. With Scott gone, you can now walk from Mar Lodge to Rothiemurchus without passing a single occupied human habitation, a distance of over 20 miles.

The bothy itself was always in good condition. A solid wooden construction, it was easy to heat from the plentiful timber around. It always had a ramshackle table and equally dilapidated chairs, with wooden bunks as an added luxury. The bothy was quite small, and not suitable for large parties. Emergency shelter could formerly be had in the abutting apartment next door, but this has been demolished. It is surprising that the Historic Monuments Commission allowed this, since it has a place in the history of Scottish mountaineering. In his *Cairngorm Commentary*, Patey tells of how he was relegated to this outhouse as a youngster on a freezing night, excluded from the fire and cameraderie in the main bothy. The large party included such luminaries as Bill Brooker, and, listening to the tales through the door, the young Patey decided to abandon Monro-bagging for the world of climbing.

Scott's was an ideal place for doing several of the Munros. Carn a Mahaim, the only Cairngorm ridge walk, which give breathtaking views of Braeriach and Cairntoul, as well as the Devil's Point, can be easily done in a day's outing. And for real masochists, there is Beinn Bhreac, surely the most boring hill in the world. The shapely Derry Cairngorm is a much more attractive proposition, and can be ascended by simply going 'across the river and into the trees' from Scott's. But primarily Scott's was the centre for the ascent of Macdui, the highest, if not the grandest, of the Cairngorms. A fine circular walk is to follow the Glen Derry path to Corrie Etchachan, ascend the steep track to Loch Etchachan, which lies at over 3000 feet, and still supports trout, and ascend thence to the summit of Macdui with its grand cairn. Legend has it that there were plans by outraged members of the Cairngorm Club to 'build up' Macdui to surpass Ben Nevis in height, but it remains Britain's second highest mountain. The return to Luibeg is by descending by Sron Riach, overlooking the crags of Corrie Sputan Dearg, the main climbing area on Macdui. At the foot of Sron Riach, the path continues down the Luibeg burn on the east side, and so back to Scott's. The walk can be done in the reverse direction, but the views are finer in the route suggested. But this walk, in either direction, is no simple stroll, and must be treated with respect and care as a true mountain walk.

Once upon a time, a party had battled up from Etchachan, and past its namesake loch, in a high wind that blew them off the path, and tired them sorely. Snow was falling by the time the summit was in sight, and there they halted for refreshment and rest. But conditions, already bad, were worsening, and soon there was a classic 'white out'. Here the snow falls so thick, and the sky is so full of it, that it takes on the appearance of a solid sheet. If combined with snow cover on the ground, earth flows into sky in a featureless continuum. All sense of direction is lost, and even gradual ascents and descents can be taken for their opposite. Most would agree that a white out is the most frightening of mountain conditions.

In such conditions a compass bearing must be taken. But the party was young and under-equipped, and there was no compass. One member had, however, read his W.H. Murray, and recalled that the great man had found his way off Cairn Toul in similar conditions, by throwing snow balls in front of him to test for cliffs. What they had forgotten was that Murray also had a compass to guide him. So off the party trod in a line, in what was thought to be a generally southerly direction, hoping to avoid the cliffs of Sputan Dearg, by seeing the snowballs disappear off them first. But it soon got so bad that the snowballs vanished as soon as they left the thrower's hand.

'A sack,' cried our literary expert, 'Somebody gies a sack.'

Somebody obliged, and the leader once again initiated the example of W.H., by throwing the sack ahead, its colour visible, even against the ubiquitous white void. Then, consternation! The sack also vanished! At this point, panic froze the party, until the leader cried: 'Haud on. Link arms and swing around in a circle, wi' me biding still. We'll find it then.'

This strategem worked, and the sack was recovered. After some further progress, inching forward after the sack, a cry of hope went up.

'Footsteps. We can follow them aff the hill!'

'Aye, ye daft gowk, but they're our ain,' was the sickening reply. The party had, unawares, gone round in a circle, contoured the hill, and were once again just below the summit. It was decided then to play safe, and set off in roughly a westerly direction; a longer route, but with no cliffs. Again the snail's pace was resumed, until luckily the party attained the Allt a Choire Mhor burn, a black ribbon against the whiteness, and began following it through a hellish boulder field. On reaching the Lairig Ghru, they had an extra five miles or so to walk home, but they were safe. And all they needed was a flickering compass needle to carry them to safety: a lesson had been learned. Though they had not panicked, and had shown a great deal of gumption, luck had undoubtedly favoured them in a way it did not favour many others in similar situations. In another similar weekend in the Lairig Ghru, several army cadets died of exposure on a training exercise.

Very often, however, fortune does not favour the brave, but the idiotic. On descending Macdui rather late on in the day, a party saw an amazing apparition ahead. A sack of fertilizer, equipped with limbs and head, was ascending. Getting near, they saw that it was a man intent on ascending the hill. To keep his clothes dry, he had removed them, and was intent on doing the hill in his underpants. To keep dry, he had fashioned a cape out of a fertiliser sack. These are ticklish situations: idiots don't like being told that's what they are, so the descending party mildly suggested that it was late, and the weather none too good. This was brushed aside, and off he trod into the mirk, blue bag visible as limbs vanished. 'There'll be nae problem finding his deid body,' commented one observer, but in fact he survived, as did another who told his story before the helicopter whisked him out to hospital from Scott's the same night. He had walked through the Lairig, and had descended to Glen Dee, when night fell, whereupon he rolled out his bag to sleep. It had become sodden, however, so he had abandoned it and descended further in the dark, passing Corrour Bothy, where he could have kept dry, had he known it existed. He staggered down Glen Lui, and at Derry Woods saw the light of Scott's bothy, and virtually crawled towards it, where shelter, warmth and food were waiting. As he revived, he seemed to think he had done rather well....

One of the beauties of Scott's was that there are plenty of low level and bad weather options, even simply strolling the woods of old Scots pine along the Luibeg or Derry. Another wee stroll is to descend the glen to the ruined clachans alongside the Lui water. After the Jacobite rebellion of 1715, led by the Earl of Mar, the estates were forfeited, and many tenants cleared from the glen, and the clearances continued until it was empty. Gaelic was spoken universally in Highland Aberdeenshire a couple of centuries back, and survived among some of the older people until after World War II. Today, glens like Derry are totally deserted, and Gaelic not spoken at all in the Cairngorm area, the patois of the locals being a broad Aberdeenshire accent. Scott himself was a good example. Though one of his parents was a Gaelic speaker, and he was partly brought up by the Gruers at Inverey, his tongue was braid Scots, whereas his predecessors at Luibeg all had the Gaelic.

A further low level walk is the Lairig an Laoigh (Pass of the Calves) which is actually longer than the more famous Lairig Ghru, though lower and less rugged. It was used for droving the younger cattle to the lowlands in bygone days. From Scott's you pass Derry Lodge, now rapidly becoming a ruin, and continue up the glen, by the good path on the west bank, which passes through one of the most lovely landscapes of river and trees in the whole Cairngorms. Experiments in Scots Pine regeneration are taking place here. You next còme to a bridge where the glen widens out to a strath, and you also come into contact with the hideous bulldozed road that comes from Mar, and goes far up into the glen. The Cairngorm area is dry and ideal for bulldozed roads, which have done so much to lessen the area's wilderness character over the past 20 years. The glen used to be dammed at this point, to allow logs to be floated down when the area was more wooded, and the strath was a summer pasture and the site of old sheilings. Where the bulldozed atrocity ends, a path heads for Corrie Etchachan, but our route continues towards the col between Beinn a Chaorainn and Beinn Mheadhoin, before descending to the Fords of Avon. From there the traveller can carry on below Bynack More, possibly visiting its weird rock tors, the Barns of Bynack, and then descending towards Rothiemurchus. If Scott's is the base, a stroll along Loch Avon to the Shelter Stone, and thence back to Glen Derry via Loch Etchachan can complete a very pleasant day.

A Luibeg regular was Desperate Dan, a late convert to mountain joys, who had a bit of catching up to do. He was the only man who ever studied for mountaineering, the way others do for exams, immersing himself in mountain memoirs and S.M.C. guides by the shelfload. By dint of his studies, his knowledge soon surpassed that of his comrades, and it was to be of great advantage, since it was he who broadened their horizons, and convinced them that they could do some of what he called the 'easier climbs'. Little did his pals realise that he had dreams of becoming one of the immortals, with them as his (possibly mortal) helpers. If anyone could typify the traits of the dour east-coaster, it was Desperate Dan. Never did a man spend so much thought on his own welfare. Tea bags were counted, and spoons weighed to lighten his pack by ounces, and other expedients were resorted to. He made sure he did not have to carry the stove or paraffin, simply by not buying a stove. In the distribution of climbing gear, it was he who officiated, and others found themselves roped and ironmongered to the floor. He would race to a bothy to get the best sleeping space, or down off a hill to get the best seat by the fire. But for broadening their horizons he could be forgiven his foibles.

However, some of Dan's wilder schemes failed to raise an echo. One such was to organise an expedition to the Lofoten Islands, to which he was convinced you could hitch-hike a lift from a trawler at the Albert Quay. He painted the attractions of such a trip in glowing colours. 'Ye can get a peak named aifter yersel — there's hunners o unclimbed anes,' he claimed. And then, lowering his voice, 'There's the weemin. The Eskimoes lock them up in the winter, and then let them oot. Tae avoid inbreeding, passing sailors and climbers can tak their pick.'

Doubts as to the very existence, never mind the sexual habits, of the Lofoten Eskimoes probably accounted for less in the undermining of this expedition than the terror inspired by pictures of the vertical Lofoten peaks.

One under-financed and under-equipped expedition finally made it to the Jotunheim Mountains in Norway, where the duo virtually starved on discovering, deep in the mountains, that those tins, the cheapest in the shop, which were to sustain them, contained catfood.

Maybe Dan's idea would have been a better one.......

'This is for us, Sputan Dearg,' said Desperate Dan, sitting in the comfy seat in the ingleneuk of Luibeg, and quoting from his treasured S.M.C. guide. *'For the novice, there is no better training ground. The rock is excellent... gets much sun'.* It sounded too good to be true, but the next day, on reaching the floor of the Corrie, even the sceptics were silenced. The climbs looked reassuringly short and easy-angled.

'Crystal Ridge, that's oor first target,' he announced, as the party trudged to the base of the cliff, and divided into groups of two. Roped up, Dan shot off nimbly on good holds to the foot of the slab. His second followed through to the next belay at the end of an arete, whereupon Dan led the last pitch to the summit. The second party accomplished the climb with similar ease.

'Ye see, I tell't ye we could dae it,' cried the vindicated Dan. 'Anchor route next!'

This, too, was accomplished with ease, as Dan babbled 'Jugs, lovely jugs a' the wye.'

Once again the occult little red tome was consulted.

'Flake Buttress next. "A splendid variety of pitches."' read out Dan, and they moved on towards it, eating on the hoof to make the most of the day's limited time. Up a chimney and slab went the first party. The second pitch then involved a traverse, achieved by reaching for a good hold, and swinging out. But as the second man in the first party reached the belay where his leader waited, a cry of distress came from below. The second party was in trouble. *De profundis* came the voice of the smallest member of the party.

'I cannae reach the hauds for the swing oot!'

Eventually they came up with a solution. The second man in the first party unroped, and held onto a flake for grim death while his leader, still belayed, lowered a 'top rope' to the party below, who were manhandled up to the now very crowded ledge. Here frantic couplings and uncouplings took place, amid spaghetti hoops of rope, resembling more an escapologist's act than a mountain climb. The first time they got it wrong, and ended up with three men on one rope, leaving the first man of the second party in splendid isolation. Eventually, however, order was restored, and they moved off, a little less confidently, to the top, where it was decided to call it a day, and a resounding success. They moved back down the glen with aching limbs, but light-heartedly garrulous.

Coming back down, they missed the bridge, and carried on the south side of the Luibeg burn. Half way back they stumbled on a magnificent dead deer, with a full set of antlers. Dan sudddenly found the energy to drop his sack and tackle the job of removing them.

'Gie's a hand. We'll get a puckle bawbees for these in Braemar!'

But his exhausted companions staggered on, too tired to help, and leaving him humphing at the antlers, foot on the beast's head. Back at Scott's some time passed without Dan's return, then they heard his footsteps, and turned to be greeted by a horrible stench, and saw Dan covered in stains.

'Ah got the damned things aff, but the brains spirked oer my claes!'

And he had nothing to change into. The stench hung in the doss, and then in the bus going home. Everyone forgot to ask what happened to the antlers....

In many ways, the best part of the day was its end, with a roaring fire in the grate, huddled round it, poring over maps of tasks done and still to be done. Wet clothes dried out, and stiff limbs relaxed in the fireglow, as craving bellies were filled with food, food that would be rejected as unpalatable elsewhere, often as not spiced with meths or paraffin. Copious cups of tea replaced lost sweat: strangely enough, parties never got 'fou and unco' happy' in bothies in those days, saving that for the beginning or end of the trip in the pub. Beer was too heavy to carry much of, and callow youth had not yet discovered that *uisge beatha* is the cure for all aches and pains, mental or physical.

In Luibeg you met all sorts, from the famed tigers, to the frenzied Munro baggers, as well as weird and wonderful eccentrics. The comrades were coming back off the hill one day, when a scene so bizarre it was almost epic greeted their eyes. The sky was heaving with black clouds, and the rain was pouring down. There, in the midst of this wilderness, was an old lady, ill-clad for the season, wielding a paintpot and brush upon the Rights of Way Society pointers which indicated the two Cairngorm Lairigs. With much difficulty she was persuaded into Scott's for a cup of tea and a heat at the fire. She sat there primly, knees close together and on the edge of her seat, as if she feared for her virtue. She made it her self-appointed task to wander the central Highlands, rather like a latter-day Old Mortality, restoring the inscriptions on the markers. 'But they pye me for my pint,' she added.

Another character who sticks in the memory is the spectacled Highlander from the Utter Hebrides, sitting crosslegged on the ground, syphoning petrol from his motorbike, and then tearing up a raw rabbit with his bare hands, to throw it in the pot. Meeting an actual *bona-fide* Highlander who frequents the mountains for pleasure is an unusual event. In conversation he committed a great *faux pas* by saying: 'I'm not liking the Cairngorm climbing. It's all chumping for chugs.'

This implication that their beloved hills required more brawn than brain to deal with, led to a shower of invective being hurled at the poor Cheuchter's head, albeit of a good-natured kind.

'Awa hame tae Invercockaleekie, if ye dinna like it here, and if yer bike will get ye that far. Yer brain's addled wi a' the petrol ye've drunk.'

'Terrible for the drink, thae cheuchters. And they're inbred as well.'

A regular visitor to Scott's was Max. Despite his lack of breeding and small size, he was always the first to the top of a hill, and always the last down. He loved Luibeg, since he could chase the chickens of an evening, and occasionally romp with Scott's own dogs. Once after a day on the hill, a crowd stood round outside Scott's in a beautiful summer's evening. Desperate Dan teased the mutt by offering him a bit of his 'piece', and then consuming it himself. The brute disappeared round the bothy, and re-appeared behind his tormentor, to stalk the object of his desire. Leaping at it, he snatched it from his owner, who then swung at the mutt with a heavy boot, only to drench himself in his tea, while the dog made off to a safe distance to consume his prize.

Another shaggy dog story concerned what must have been the record ascent of Ben Macdui. Two collie dogs attached themselves to a man who started from Luibeg up the mountain.   But every time the man stopped to rest, one of the dogs would bark and snarl, till progress was resumed.   Unable to stop even at the summit for fear of a savaging, food was consumed on the move, to the accompaniment of snarls every time a stop was even contemplated.   It is doubtful if Collie himself retreated faster off Macdui when pursued by the Fearlach Mor (Grey Man) than that man pursued by the collies.   At Luibeg the dogs were reclaimed by a shepherd, who seemed to be accustomed to such escapades.

Of the Gray Man, a sort of Macdui Yeti, little seems to have been seen in recent years, though the Brocken Spectre phenomenon, when the climber is stalked by a giant shadow, is a not uncommon one on the higher reaches of the hill.

In its latter years, Scott's gave the appearance of being more used than formerly, when it was largely the reserve of the Aberdeen Mafia, possibly since it made a convenient stopping-off place point for 'doing' the Cairngorm Lairigs.   On a recent sentimental return visit, it was chock full of an English party.   Nice lads, and on the 'wine of the country', but they had never heard of Scott and knew nothing of the bothy's history.   Carefully laid bait led to the solicited question.

'You've been here before, then?'

'Listen, young man, I set eyes on yon antifreeze advert above the lum there afore ye were born.'

And an evening of pleasant patter was initiated, where older hearts warmed to see that the youngsters were willing to listen to tales told a few times, but hardly the same way twice.   Scott and Max may have gone to the great hill in the sky, but bothies can still provide for new generations the delights they once did for us.

Red Deer Stag

A WINTER'S DAY

Cold dawn. It was December, and in the hut a bar of pale light from an east-facing window filtered through dust and dirt to reveal four figures entombed in their sleeping bags. Though awake, they did not move. Even in their drowsing state they were aware of a tension in their minds, and that, when added to an awareness of the waiting chill, created a deep reluctance to emerge and face what was to be done that day.

Soon, however, three of them became aware of the fourth moving. The floorboards creaked to the sudden movement of the body unzipping the sleeping bag. Then accompanied by the sound of human awakening, the clearing of the throat, snuffling, the stretching, the odd groan, a long yawn, the lie-abeds heard the rustle of swift dressing. Suddenly those rather muted sounds were replaced by a harsher cacophony — the vibram soles of solid boots on the bare floorboards, the rattle of metal dishes and cutlery being moved aside as the big drum for tea was picked up.   It all ended with the thump of the closing door — silence again, but only for as long at it took the 'Big Yin' to walk the few paces to the burn, burst through the crust of ice that had formed overnight, and fill the drum with water. The pleasant drowiness was replaced by a more waking state as the Big Yin returned to clump around, lighting the stove and selecting the least dirty of the pans from the filthy detritus of kitchenware in order to prepare breakfast. The sleepers would now have to move.

Yet their movements were not those of the quick and eager. First, one by one, they sat up, rubbed their faces and blinked bleary-eyed at the tall lean figure now huddled over a frying pan, probing a reluctant sausage with a finger of dubious cleanliness. It could be seen then that this was not an all-male gathering, for one of the slow risers was the Big Yin's new wife. It was she who spoke the first words of the day.

'What about some bacon? There's some in my pack.'

Her husband leaned over, pulled the pack towards him and rummaged about until he found the packet. He opened it and threw the contents into the pan. After that, not much else was said. Breakfast was eaten in silence, its participants often staring into space, their minds caught in a dwam. There was not much to say. It had all been discussed the night before as they had prepared for bed. They were going up the hill, but not to climb. They had something else in mind.

After breakfast the usual preparations were made. Bad weather gear and some food were stuffed into their packs. Then the Big Yin left the hut and walked out onto the moor behind. From the way he walked, the angle of his body, it could be seen he was looking for something. Suddenly, after to-ing and fro-ing for a while his pace quickened. He had found it, and stooping down he began to remove turf, heather and stones from the secret cache. Standing up, he pulled out a long object wrapped in polythene and canvas from the excavation he had made.

The Big Yin returned to the hut, where he began to open up the parcel to reveal its contents. It was in perfect condition despite having spent some time in the deep, damp bowels of the moor. Its wooden butt and steel barrel gleamed with the oils used to protect them. The Big Yin assembled those two parts with a long tool found in the parcel, and then tried out the weapon. The trigger gave a dry click. It seemed to be working satisfactorily. From a smaller parcel he produced the ammunition — .303, suitable for killing red deer.

166

The others sat quietly and looked at the rifle.   They had never been so close to such a thing before, and knew very little about the stalking and killing of deer.   They were apprehensive, to say the least.   That is to say, the two males were apprehensive.   The female, Big Yin's new wife, sat in silent admiration of the scene being played out in front of her.   She had married a real man, a man of action, and not some limp-wristed wimp.   For her then, this was just fine.

The two young lads were not so sure, but their reservations remained in the realm of silent reluctance.   They were the junior partners in this situation, for the Big Yin dominated by his age and his elevated position in the world of climbing.   They could not withdraw, for not only would it have incurred the wrath of the Big Yin, but their claim to be 'two of the boys' would have been placed in some jeopardy.

If it wasn't that he had to maintain his hard man's image, the Big Yin would perhaps have admitted to feeling at least a *frisson* of fear. After all, it was his first solo attempt at putting something in the pot.   He had, of course, served his apprenticeship with the old crowd, and they had been sufficiently impressed to allow him access to one of their guns.

They were men you did not mess with.   Silent and secretive, strong and hard.   They used to appear in the small hours of the morning after spending a night on the river, dodging gamekeepers, sometimes fighting with them, their packs full of salmon — silver bars they used to call them.   Where they got their guns nobody knew, and nobody asked.   It would have seemed indelicate to have done so.   That is perhaps what worried the young team.   Whilst this venture held out the promise of entry into the freemasonry of the 'old crowd', they could not deny to themselves the obvious dangers.   Were they ready for it?   There no longer seemed time to ask questions.

'Here's what we'll dae.'   The Big Yin broke the silence.   'Jean'll drive us up onto the moor.'   At this point he nodded towards his two reluctant acolytes.   'We'll do a big swing round to the west, an' see if we cannae get something.'   As there was nothing else to do but agree, they picked up their packs and shuffled out into the cold day.   You could not tell the Big Yin you didn't like the taste of venison.   Nor was he the kind of fellow who would be impressed with arguments about animal rights.

Up on the moor, as the noise of the van receded in the blustery wind, the three men made their way across the heather.   It was early, and at that moment, it was one of those clear bright days when the atmosphere is cleansed by intermittent showers, and although the oblique light from the east made sharp the image of peat bog and heather tussock, there was enough cloud around to suggest that before the day was out there could be some nasty, wintery squalls.   The light dusting of fresh snow on the moor confirmed that impression.

New to this game, the hunters did not know what to expect.   They thought, however, they would have to find the deer and then stalk them carefully before getting in a shot.   That would probably involve moving deep into the moor.   In fact, the action started almost immediately, for only a hundred yards from the road half a dozen or so hinds suddenly appeared as if from a trap door in the moor.   Despite the presence of passing cars on the nearby road, the Big Yin dropped onto one knee, raised the rifle butt to his shoulder and blasted off two or three shots.   The resulting sharp cracks returned as thunder that rolled around the surrounding hills and corries.

In the silence that followed the three men watched the white tails of the unharmed deer run over the moor towards a high corrie.   The Big Yin needed some target practice.   This was certainly the opinion of wee John, for during the short walk from the road he had managed to get himself in front (though luckily to the right) of the other two.   When the shooting started he had flung himself to the ground, which was just as well, for the bullets, he claimed, had passed uncomfortably close to his head.   Like the deer, though for different reasons, John was unimpressed with the Big Yin's shooting ability.   He was not, however, an excitable or demonstrative man.   He merely stood up, and, brushing the snow, peat and heather from his clothes, announced grimly but quietly that he did not propose to continue with this expedition. As he brushed by them, without another word, the other two did not try to stop him or argue with him. They seemed to realise that John's experience had created in him a justifiable fear of the bullet that removed him from the pressures that had led him to embark on this adventure.

When the tension of the moment passed, the remaining two men turned their attention to the fleeing beasts. They had gone off towards the high corrie of an adjacent hill which was capped with the solid snows of winter. If the deer had entered the corrie it seemed likely that they would be trapped, for they would not be too happy about climbing above the snowline. Following this line of reasoning, the Big Yin shouldered his rifle, barrel down so as not to present a provocative profile to any watching gamekeeper, and urged his companion to proceed with him in pursuit of the deer.

It took some time to reach and climb into the corrie. It was not only the distance that had to be covered, but also the roughness of the ground that made progress difficult. It was wild peat bogs, treacherously muddy at the bottom, topped by coarse grass and heather. Moreover there was a need for stealth, for the beasts were on edge. Someone out there was trying to kill them. It was the Big Yin, undeterred by his wild firing, enthusiastic as ever to get in close enough to have another shot.

This he eventually did — two of them. But once again his aim was defective, and, to the accompaniment of the rolling thunder of the shots, the deer, agile and sure of foot on the rough terrain, half-circled their would-be killer before descending into the narrow glen below. They did not stop until they had crossed the wide river and the road to gain the slopes of the mountain on the other side. Once again the men followed, the Big Yin keen as ever for the kill, his companion growing visibly less enthusiastic. His mood was reflected in the deteriorating weather, for the once blue skies had now been replaced by low black clouds that stalked slowly down and around the surrounding hills. It looked and felt as though it was going to snow.

The rapid descent of a steep hillside made rough by boulder and bog is no easy task. The co-ordination of muscle and sinew requires intense concentration, and a moment's lapse can result in a stumble that could damage the legs of the most seasoned of mountain men. Accordingly, the two men were giving a great deal of attention to the placing of their feet. There was, however, time enough to give a glance at the narrow road towards which they were rushing. And just as well, for into the jolting consciousness of the mad descent came the vision of what they most feared — the Land Rover — brown/green to blend with its normal surroundings, but now picked out as a black silhouette against the light covering of snow.

Time only to lurch down into a peat hag and lie hard against its crumbling wall before the Land Rover stopped to spill out its gamekeepers, predictable in their coarse tweed jackets and plus fours. They had heard the thunder in the hills and had come to investigate, armed with telescope and rifle. And so while they stood braced against the vehicle, long telescopes to their eyes, the hunters remained hidden. One was on his back, looking at the black clouds above, the other glowering over the tussocks at the forces that lay between him and his quarry. Both were cursing this intrusion, but were doing so for different reasons. The Big Yin saw his pot remaining empty: his companion did not trust the Big Yin to give up easily. 'Christ,' he thought, 'What would happen now? If they come after us, there's not much in the way of alternatives. Back up into the corrie and up over the hill? In the winter, with a short day and the weather deteriorating, there's not much over there, just moors, hills and more moors. What's the other choice? The Big Yin will fight it out! Oh, Christ, gunfight at the OK corrie! A shooting war! That's serious! That's gaol! Aw naw!' Dread thoughts, accompanied now by eyes turned heavenwards, forced to blink by the first few heavy, wet snowflakes of an approaching mess of weather.

Thus lay the hunters, bodies inert, trapped by authorities' field of vision. Minds in movement, though, concentrating on potential action if there was any hostile advance. Twenty minutes, thirty minutes they lay there, uneasy bedfellows in their tense ruminations.

The clouds were getting blacker, the snow was getting thicker, and dim light blurred the images of their pursuers. The dampness slunk through their clothes, yet fear kept them fixed to the wet peat. But suddenly the gamekeepers had had enough. They dropped their telescopes to their sides, climbed into their vehicle, and drove off in the direction they were facing, the wheels cutting black lines in the fresh fallen snow.

The relief of tension and the joy of resumed downward movement tempered, for a few moments anyway, the other's realisation that the Big Yin was not to be put off by the knowledge that the gamies were onto him. He wanted a beast, and there were six of them on the mountain on the other side of the glen. He had a reputation for being a ruthless and tenacious climber, qualities that now motivated the hunter. So down again, slipping, sliding, jolting on the rough wet surface. Down and across the river shrunk by frost, and then up again. Up onto the road. 'The tracks! What about the tracks?' Clear, perfect images of vibram soles in the wet snow. Evidence of their dishonourable intentions.

'Leave them. There's nuthin' we can do. Maybe the snow'll cover them.'

This time a proper stalk. Careful, bellies down in peaty mud, cold wet clothes sticking to chilled bodies. But they did not notice. Concentration was fixed firmly on the deer. When they seemed to be not looking their way, the hunters would move briskly from one peat hag to another. They were getting closer. The deer looked round suspiciously and sniffed at the air as if to catch a smell of the assassins. Then lowering their heads they grazed briefly again, only to lift their heads once more. They were nervous, and rightly so. They could not see or smell the malevolence, but they knew it was there.

How long this subtle persecution went on it is difficult to know. In the concentration required by the hunters to control breathing and movement, awareness of time evaporates. For the hinds, time already had no meaning. For them, there are only seasons of survival, and now this wicked winter held a new terror. In this way hinds and men stayed locked together in a slow waltz of death across the lower slopes of the mountain. The deer were edgy and suspicious, ready to dash to safety, yet wishing to conserve dwindling supplies of energy. The men were determined to find the weaknesses to breach the defences of that suspicion, eager to get close enough to have a shot.

Suddenly, the chance came. One beast, a little behind the others, with an unexpected and careless nonchalance, wheeled around to present a profile too good to miss. The big Yin snapped up onto one knee and fired two shots. The inevitable cracks of doom rang out scarcely muffled by the snow. Yet they did not herald death, for once again the Big Yin's aim proved to be defective. As he watched the white tails disappear into the gathering gloom he was overwhelmed by emotion. Appalled, disgusted at his lack of success, he cursed the rifle, and the weather and the deer. His companion said nothing. He was thinking that surely they must give up now. It was getting late and the gloom was beginning to coagulate into a solid darkness. And anyway that bloody Land Rover might come back.

He was right in both things. They were well on their way down when the Land Rover arrived back on the road. The previous performance was repeated, but this time the hunters were hidden so close to the road that, even though there was little light, they could make out the features of the gamekeepers. They recognised them, because they had seen them in the public bar of the local hotel. They had even played darts with them. Luckily, the deep gloom of the late winter afternoon hid the tracks the hunters had made in the snow, and also it seemed that their erstwhile drinking companions were not too enthusiastic about pursuing their duties on such a cold and miserable night, for soon they all packed up their telescopes, clambered aboard their vehicle and drove off.

Surely that must be the end. But it was not. On the way back, near the hut, a huge stag emerged from out of the moor, and the Big Yin was off again, stumbling through the dusk, trying to organise his rifle. This time, the chase was short. The stag, stronger than his female counterparts, did not hang around long enough to attract lead from the Big Yin. He disappeared, leaving the Big Yin to fumble helplessly with his weapon. It was all over now. There was nothing left to do but to return the rifle to its hiding place and go back to the hut.

There, the fire was on. Jean and wee John were sitting in the flickering light waiting for their return. No meal was being prepared, for they were awaiting the liver from the kill. As the mighty hunters stripped off their wet clothes, they told of their failure. Without a word to express the obvious disappointment, packs were opened. Perhaps there were some sausages left.

'Aye, there's some.'

'An' tattie scones.'

'Good. That'll be grand.'

'Get the tea on!'

Later, sitting staring at the flames the way people do, warmed by the tea and reclining on sleeping bags, the story of the hunt was recounted. 'Maybe there's something wrong with the sight,' said Jean. She had not been married long enough to think that her man was anything less than perfect.

'Maybe,' agreed the Big Yin. Yet he was not going to let it get him down. There would be other times and things could only get better. Meantime there was tonight to look forward to. The thought amused him so he shared it with the others. 'It'll be a right laugh the night down at the pub drinking with those dumb bastards that were out looking for us the day. They've no' got a clue, huv they?'

The Table

A WINTER'S NIGHT

'It's still snowing.'

The speaker moved back into the bothy, revealing, briefly, the whirling storm outside, before a shower of oaths led to a rapid re-closing of the door.

Still snowing. It was snowing on the high mosses, turning them from velvet to ermine: it was snowing on the slopes, hiding the contours of the great boulder fields. It fell and drifted in the glens, obliterating paths, and it was driven into the corries high above. On the lochans, it was 'a moment white — then melts forever.' The Scots pine clumps were sinking in the morass.

Deer had slunk down to the habitations of men, where they might find food and shelter. But a party of men, in hopes for the morrow, had abandoned the dwellings of their fellows, and headed through worsening weather to this mountain refuge. Long before their arrival, the snow had begun to fall, and hours later it was still falling in earnest — soft powder snow.

In winter, everything becomes more intense by several powers. Ground conditions are tougher, and packs necessarily heavier with winter gear. Days are shorter; there is no time to rest, and the cold generally prevents this, anyway. Energy is expended quicker, and exhaustion a threat. Sometimes nature can take pity and help. A good frost can provide a footing across which you fly as if on wings. But most often this is not the case. Melting snow is a curse, no longer able to bear the body, which sinks through at every weary step. But the worst of all is deep powder snow. This will not support the body at all, and the climber must go through it like a snow plough. It is cruelly exhausting work.

175

The snow was already deep, and by morning would be waist-high. There would be no possibility of going up the hill. Even a retreat down the valley would be a major expedition.

And it was still snowing.

Morale was low, lower than the temperature inside the howff, and falling. The weekend, the precious weekend, snatched from the surrounding days of reluctant toil, was a disaster. The time in preparation, packing, purchasing supplies, and the costs of the journey, were all wasted. No-one moved, rather they sat in sweat-dampened clothes in the cold, and in silence. Finally a bitter voice broke the silence.

'I could've been at haim, in front of the fire, instead of here, freezing my doup aff.'

'You'd have been at haim, bairns screaming, telly blaring, and your wife turning doun the fire to save money......If you weren't here, you wouldn't appreciate haim!'

The description of the first speaker's domestic disharmony did little to cheer him up and make him reappraise his position. He muttered disconsolately: 'If that was the case, I could appreciate haim by sleeping in the lobby or the backie.'

Silence fell again. Then scufflings and scramblings in a corner by one of the party led to certain others enquiring, in no gentle terms, as to the purpose of the disturbance. But the ice on even the hardest heart there thawed a little at the sight of a bottle held aloft, inside which, in spite of the gloom, gleamed a pale amber liquid. 'I was keeping this for the morn, to celebrate. But there's nae point now. Let's get stuck intae it.'

Mugs clanked against glass as the nectar passed round: as one spirit sank, others rose. One or two were sufficiently cheered to remove boots and wet clothes; a candle or two appeared, and were positioned in nooks and crannies, giving a cheer to the howff. 'Let's get a bile on,' said one, and while he assembled a primus stove, another filled the dixies with snow, to melt for a brew. Sacks were unpacked, sleeping bags rolled out and padded with spare clothes against the floor. The chill was retreating from the bothy, and from the hearts of those who were were taking possession of it.

'Still,' a mildly mollified malcontent proffered, If it's nae tae appreciate the delights of haim, what on earth is the point of the pain, the cold, the discomfort the.....' and the wave of a mildly inebriated hand conveyed all the wordless horror in his mind. Again silence fell for a while.

'Women.' This word drew attention to its utterer, a hitherto silent observer of the proceedings. 'It's women, to get awa fae them. In your youth you want to escape your mither and all her nonsense and fuss. Then fan you're a teenager, it's to escape lassies, and be with your pals. Now it's wives, and their carry-ons, you want to get away frae, and get peace for once.'

A stunned silence greeted this mysogenistic tirade, uttered with a finality that brooked no opposition. Someone finally offered a jocular alternative view. 'It's just the opposite: it's tae get women. It's the hope that on the bus some young lovely will be lured tae the bothy, or that fan you get there, it'll be full of lusty wenches.'

Ribald outbursts greeted this analysis, which found theoretical favour. Tales were then told of bothy books indicating the departure of a female party just before the arrival of young bloods. Then one character spoke. 'I remember once...' But as ears pricked up, he hesitated, seemed to think better of it, and lapsed into silence. An embarrassed hush fell over the company, minds turning to similar paths, about which the passing of youth had removed the desire to brag and boast.

In the conversational hiatus, most returned to unpacking of gear. Coiled ropes slithered like serpents into corners, and food, glorious food, was piled onto the table.

Then a cry of horror pierced the flickering gloom. 'What in the name of Heaven is that?' One man suddenly found himself the object of general attention as he stood, with a gas stove in his hand, uncomprehending.

'Great God, it's a gas stove.   It's a dreadful thing, the gas.   Paraffin stoves are cheaper tae run, give a better heat, and what's more, they're traditional.   I'm sick of seeing empty gas containers littering the hills.'

'You're living in the days of tweed jackets and nailed boots.   And as for that Alpenstock of yours....'

Here general laughter greeted the indication of an ice axe of larger than normal size, lying linseed oil-soaked in the corner.

'Great deeds have been done with such implements: they distinguish a man.   They bring a sense of stablility and tradition, like Ordnance Survey maps that cost three shillings and sixpence, and old S.M.C. guides with the pictures that look sepia toned.'

He would have continued in his favourite, half-serious vein, but news that a 'Bile' had been obtained brought a halt to the altercation. However, this only served to drive the custodian of tradition into a new mock frenzy.

'Tea bags?   What do you expect a man to get his teeth into? Chewing the leaf is the best part of a bile.   But what can you expect nowadays.....'

The whisky was doing its rounds with the tea, and the howff was getting quite cosy.   The paraffin stoves were left on, and soon glowed red-hot, driving out the cold.   Tradition, at least here, was vindicated, and the party was not spared the point.

A man was dunking a thoughtful biscuit (the carob coated oatmeal of maturity in place of the careless chocolate digestive of his youth) into his tea.   Watching the object go limp in the mug, he found inspiration.

'I think it's to do with your self-image.   You want to see yourself cast in a certain mould.   When you start it's because you think you're Hemingway, and Big Two Hearted River stuff.   Then you see yourself as a new Patey, fighting the good fight, and triumphing, on

178

new routes in blizzards, with holes in your boots. When you find you can't do this, you adopt a more reflective role, a gentleman climber, chipping at geological specimens, and dabbling in Gaelic place-names. Our alpenstock man sees himself that way.'

Some general thought was given to this in the pre-prandial imbibing that was taking place. Then a unilateral verdict was offered.

'That can't be it. Because you very quickly realise that you won't be able to write like Hemingway, that mild V.-Diff is about your standard of climbing, and you lack the money to be a gentleman climber. *They* had the right idea, now — country seats and hotels, hot baths and venison steaks.....'

Mention of venison steaks took minds temporarily off the debate, and on to the preparation of the evening meal. The table was gravid with grub. Piles of tins of meat, heaps of vegetables, loaves galore and pots of honey — all invited hunger.

'Look at that!' said one, examining the cornucopia. 'And to think that an apple and a packet of soup was enough in the days of the Big Two Hearted River.'

But on examining a packet of breakfast cereal his tone changed.

'What's this? Brecky-Wecky, or some damned rat food? You can't expect a man to go on the hill in mid-winter with that! You need a good bellyfull of cholesterol in the guts first — tattie scones, dumpling, and black pudding with lots of ingans. Who's responsible? What man committed this gastronomic atrocity?'

However, hunger had overtaken the pleasures of baiting the defender of tradition. 'Belt up, you cantankerous old fart, and get that tin of corned beef and tatties on. There's an ingan as well.'

Soon the only sounds heard were the sizzling of frying onions and the bubble of boiling potatoes. As the tang of the food spread, bellies discovered in an instant that they were empty, and wished on the stove. The montane museum attendant, in charge of producing the meal, reckoned this allowed him the luxury of one last barb.

'It'd be morning afore we ate, if it was the gas stoves we were using.'

Finally the hash was handed round in generous amounts, and little was heard but the scrape of knife on dixie, and the contented murmur of mastication. Uncleansed utensils were discharged into corners, and the feasters stretched out in a state of replete satisfaction.

'Where's that damn whisky? Has prohibition started again?'

'It's easy seen you didnae carry it in — or pay for it,' came the reply, but the bottle came with it.

'The satisfaction you give your pals should be payment enough', and he took a hefty swig to show how seriously he took the granting of such satisfaction.

The whisky, the food, the gentle light and the growing camaraderie had a benign effect on more than one mind. In this temporary euphoria, it was inevitable that selective memory should begin to work, and that someone would turn romantic and idealistic. 'There's things that can only be experienced here,' said one who had not yet proffered a solution to the riddle that puzzled them all.

'Aye, sair feet!' quipped a cynic. But the speaker carried on as if possessed.

'Things that the complacent self-satisfied oafs and slobs we spend our lives with can never share or even imagine......Walking into Barrisdale Bay on an ink-black night when the stars come out and the moon shows you the fjord as clear as day. Morning on a perfect, iron-cold winter's day on the Rannoch Moor, the snow near blinding you. The Hebrides, the Isles of the Blessed, in the haze of a summer's day from the Cuillin Ridge. Experiences like that remain with you all your life.'

'I thought W.H. Murray had gone out of fashion, but here's German Romanticism alive and well.' This was quipped in a kindly tone, since a chord had been struck in the hearers.

'The trouble is, that doesn't explain it either. The experiences you mention happen a handful of times in a lifetime. Nine times out of ten you plouter through mist, soaked, feet wet, and your muscles screaming for mercy. You're glad when the day is over and you can get stuck into the grub and into your sack.'

As dixies, stoves and gear were clattered into corners, and preparations for repose took over, the desire to talk still manifested itself. Amid meticulous preparation of sleeping places, sacks serving as pillows, clothes spaced to cushion points of anatomical contact with the ground, the theme was carried on. One of the party went to relieve nature, and on opening the door, commented: 'It's still snowing.'

But this time the comment aroused little resentment, or even interest; they were absorbed in the discussion.

'It's nothing as psychological or philosophical as all this we've been hearing. It's quite simple: our lives are miserable and mediocre. All we face is frustration and failure. We come here to get away from it all, to forget it, and put ourselves in a position where we face achievable objectives. Getting to the bothy dry, keeping warm, doing the hill or the climb. It gives a false, transient sense of purpose and achievement.'

This rather put a damper on things, especially as it was followed by the extinguishing of the stoves. Their reassuring hiss was replaced by the rising wind howling outside. The candles guttered, and seemed about to be engulfed in gloom. Final preparations were made for rest: glasses and watches put in boots to avoid breakage, food hung up to discourage the mice, torches laid handy for any nocturnal trips outside. As the party tightened their sacks to keep out the cold, a final guess was offered to the great mystery.

'All the things that have been mentioned are true in part, but none is the real reason, at least as a man grows older. You come for the banter, the cameraderie, the tale-telling, the rituals of bothy life. The hill is an alibi. In the end, the bothy nights are as important as the mountain days. Now, let's get to sleep. You never know, there might be a hard frost, and it might stop snowing.'

The state of lying in comfort and security in a tiny cocoon, while outwith the walls there rages a storm that would mean death in minutes, is akin to re-entering the womb, and generally induces sleep.

In the morning it had stopped snowing, but the result of the blizzard was four feet of unconsolidated snow.   So they built snowmen, and went home early.

And some the war of attrition finally wore down.   The bad days took their toll, as did the debilitating trivia and minutiae of everyday living.   But with a few, it didn't.   They fought the good fight, even though they knew they were losing.   The last of the mountain Mohicans carried on: *The breed of men who can't stay still, the breed of men who never will*, though grey began to show in their hair, and their bodies grew heavier.   If you meet such, make a space by the fire, give them a dram, and lend them an ear.   And characters the like of Black Rab, Malky the Alky, Stumpy and Desperate Dan will once again be rejuvenated, 'forever young.'

LUATH PRESS

GUIDES TO SCOTLAND

SOUTH WEST SCOTLAND. Tom Atkinson. A guide book to the best of Kyle, Carrick, Galloway, Dumfries-shire, Kirkcudbrightshire and Wigtownshire. This lovely land of hills, moors and beaches is bounded by the Atlantic and the Solway. Steeped in history and legend, still unspoiled, it is not yet widely known. Yet it is a land whose peace and grandeur are at least comparable to the Highlands.

Legends, history and loving description by a local author make this an essential book for all who visit -- or live in -- the country of Robert Burns.

ISBN 0 946487 04 9. Paperback. £3:50p.

THE LONELY LANDS. Tom Atkinson. A guide book to Inveraray, Glencoe, Loch Awe, Loch Lomond, Cowal, the Kyles of Bute, and all of Central Argyll.

All the glories of Argyll are described in this book. From Dumbarton to Campbeltown there is a great wealth of beauty. It is a quiet and a lonely land, a land of history and legend, a land of unsurpassed glory. Tom Atkinson describes it all, writing with deep insight of the land he loves. There could be no better guide to its beauties and history. Every visitor to this country of mountains and lochs and lonely beaches will find that enjoyment is enhanced by reading this book.

ISBN 0 946847 10 3. Paperback. Price £3:50p.

ROADS TO THE ISLES. Tom Atkinson. A guide book to Scotland's far north and west, including Ardnamurchan, Morvern, Morar, Moidart, and all the west coast to Ullapool.

This is the area lying to the west and north of Fort William. It is a land of still unspoiled loveliness, of mountain, loch and silver sands. It is a vast, quiet land of peace and grandeur. Legend, history and vivid description by an author who loves the area and knows it intimately make this a book essential to all who visit this Highland wonderland.

ISBN 0 946487 01 4. Paperback. £3:25p.

THE EMPTY LANDS. Tom Atkinson. A guide book to the north of Scotland, from Ullapool to Bettyhill, and from Bonar Bridge to John O' Groats.

This is the fourth book in the series, and it covers that vast empty quarter leading up to the north coast. These are the Highlands of myth and legend, a land of unsurpassed beauty, where sea and mountain mingle in majesty and grandeur. As in his other books, the author is not content to describe the scenery (which is really beyond description) or advise you where to go. He does all that with his usual skill and enthusiasm, but he also places that superb landscape into its historical context, and tells how it and the people who live there have become what we see today. With love and compassion, and some anger, he has written a book which should be read by everyone who visits or lives in -- or even dreams about -- that empty land.

ISBN 0 946487 13 8. Paperback. £3:50p.

HIGHWAYS AND BYWAYS IN MULL AND IONA.

Peter Macnab. In this newly revised guidebook to Mull and Iona, Peter Macnab takes the visitor on a guided tour of the two islands. Born and grown up on Mull, he has an unparalleled knowledge of the island, and a great love for it. There could be no better guide than him to those two accessible islands of the Inner Hebrides, and no-one more able to show visitors the true Mull and Iona.

ISBN 0 946487 16 2. Paperback. £3:25p.

WALKS IN THE CAIRNGORMS. Ernest Cross. The

Cairngorms are the highest uplands in Britain, and walking there introduces you to sub-arctic scenery found nowhere else. This book provides a selection of walks in a splendid and magnificent countryside -- there are rare birds, animals and plants, geological curiosities, quiet woodland walks, unusual excursions in the mountains. Ernest Cross has written an excellent guidebook to those things. Not only does he have an intimate knowledge of what he describes, but he loves it all deeply, and this shows.

ISBN 0 946487 09 X. Paperback. £2:75p.

THE SPEYSIDE HOLIDAY GUIDE. Ernest Cross. Toothache in Tomintoul? Golf in Garmouth? Whatever your questions about Speyside, Ernest Cross has the answer in this Guide Book. Speyside is Scotland's ideal holiday centre. It has everything from the sub-arctic heights of the Cairngorms to the seemingly endless -- and quiet -- beaches. With a great wealth of peaceful towns and villages, it also possesses vast empty and open spaces, delightful to walk, a treasure to be discovered.

Ernest Cross knows and loves it all. In this book he directs you and guides you to the best of it. With his usual incisive wit and language, he introduces you to Scotland's most interesting area, and ensures that everyone, whether visitor or resident, is enriched by learning its secrets.

ISBN 0 946487 27 8. Paperback. £4:95p.

SHORT WALKS IN THE CAIRNGORMS. Ernest Cross.
A variety of shorter walks in the glorious scenery of the Cairngorms. It may be that you seek a stroll to the pub after dinner, or a half day on the high tops, or a guided two-hour walk round a loch. This book has them all, in profusion. You will be ably guided, and your guide will point out the most interesting sights and the best routes.

ISBN 0 946487 23 5. Paperback. £2:75p.

OTHER BOOKS FROM LUATH PRESS

TALES OF THE NORTH COAST. Alan Temperley and the pupils of Farr Secondary School. In this collection of 58 tales, there is a memorial to the great tradition of Highland story-telling. Simply told and unadorned, these tales are wide-ranging -- historical dramas, fairy tales, great battles, ship-wreck and ghosts, Highland rogues -- they all appear in this gallimaufry of tales, many of which have been told and re-told for generations round the fireside.

In addition to the tales, Alan Temperley has collected together a series of contemporary writings about the Clearances of Strathnaver, a central feature of local history, and a tragedy whose effects are still felt and discussed.

ISBN 0 946487 18 9 Paperback. £5:95.

POEMS TO BE READ ALOUD. *A Victorian Drawing Room Entertainment.* Selected and with an Introduction by Tom Atkinson. A very personal collection of poems specially selected for all those who believe that the world is full of people who long to hear you declaim such as these. The Entertainment ranges from an unusual and beautiful *Love Song* translated from the Sanskrit, to the drama of *The Shooting of Dan McGrew* and *The Green Eye of the Little Yellow God,* to the bathos of *Trees* and the outrageous bawdiness of *Eskimo Nell.* Altogether, a most unusual and amusing selection.

ISBN 0 946487 00 6. Paperback. £3:00p.

HIGHLAND BALLS AND VILLAGE HALLS. G.W. Lockhart. There is no doubt about Wallace Lockhart's love of Scottish country dancing, nor of his profound knowledge of it. Reminiscence, anecdotes, social commentary and Scottish history, tartan and dress, prose and verse, the steps of the most important dances -- they are all brought together to remind, amuse and instruct the reader in all facets of Scottish country dancing. Wallace Lockhart practices what he preaches. He grew up in a house where the carpet was constantly being lifted for dancing, and the strains of country dance music have thrilled him in castle and village hall. He is the leader of the well known *Quern Players*, and he composed the dance *Eilidh MacIain,* which was the winning jig in the competition held by the Edinburgh Branch of the Royal Scottish Country Dance Society to commemorate its sixtieth anniversary.

ISBN 0 96487 12 X Paperback. £3:95p.

THE CROFTING YEARS. Francis Thompson. A remarkable and moving study of crofting in the Highlands and Islands. It tells of the bloody conflicts a century ago when the crofters and their families faced all the forces of law and order, and demanded a legal status and security of tenure, and of how gunboats cruised the Western Isles in Government's classic answer. Life in the crofting townships is described with great insight and affection. Food, housing, healing and song are all dealt with. But the book is no nostalgic longing for the past. It looks to the future and argues that crofting must be carefully nurtured as a reservoir of potential strength for an uncertain future.

Frank Thompson lives and works in Stornoway. His life has been intimately bound up with the crofters, and he well knows of what he writes.

ISBN 0 946487 06 5. Paperback. £5:95p.

TALL TALES FROM AN ISLAND. Peter Macnab. These tales come from the island of Mull, but they could just as well come from anywhere in the Highlands and Islands. Witches, ghosts, warlocks and fairies abound, as do stories of the people, their quiet humour and their abiding wit. A book to dip into, laugh over, and enthuse about. Out of this great range of stories a general picture emerges of an island people, stubborn and strong in adversity, but warm and co-operative and totally wedded to their island way of life. It is a clear picture of a microcosmic society perfectly adapted to an environment that, in spite of its great beauty, can be harsh and unforgiving.

Peter Macnab was born and grew up on Mull, and he knows and loves every inch of it. Not for him the 'superiority' of the incomer who makes joke cardboard figures of the island people and their ways. He presents a rounded account of Mull and its people.

ISBN 0 946487 07 3. Paperback. £6:50p.

BARE FEET AND TACKETY BOOTS. Archie Cameron. The author is the last survivor who those who were born and reared on the island of Rhum in the days before the First World War, when the island was the private playground of a rich absentee landowner. Archie recalls all the pleasures and pains of those days. He writes of the remarkable characters, not least his own father, who worked the estate and guided the Gentry in their search for stags and fish. The Gentry have left ample records of their time on the island, but little is known of those who lived and worked there. Archie fills this gap. He recalls the pains and pleasures of his boyhood. Factors and Schoolmasters, midges and fish, deer and ducks and shepherds, the joys of poaching, the misery of MacBraynes' steamers -- they are all here.

This book is an important piece of social history, but, much more, it is a fascinating record of a way of life gone not so long ago, but already almost forgotten.

ISBN 0 946487 17 0. Paperback. £5:95p

THE BOTHY BREW. Hamish Brown. Hamish Brown is well known as a writer on Scottish, travel and outdoor subjects, as a photographer, lively lecturer, and editor of two poetry anthologies. His short stories have appeared in a wide range of publications.

H.e has climbed and travelled extensively in the Alps and less-known areas of Europe as well as in the remote Andes and Himalayas and each year spends some months in the south of Morocco. When not busy travelling and writing, home is at Kinghorn, with a view over the Forth to Edinburgh.

Although already the author of a dozen or so books, most of them reflecting his interest in and concern for the outdoors of Scotland, this is Hamish Brown's first collection of short stories.

This collection shows a remarkable range of interests and enthusiasms. They range from a murder on a beach at midnight to a family picnic at Loch Lomond, from a search for Painted Ladies in the mountains of Morocco to a search for a cuckoo in the Scottish hills.

These stories, although easy and a delight to read, yet show Hamish Brown's deep love for Scotland and the hills, and his profound knowledge of Scotland today.

ISBN 0 946 487 26 X. Paperback. Prince: £5:95p.

COME DUNGEONS DARK. John Caldwell. The Life and Times of Guy Aldred, Glasgow Anarchist. Hardly a street-corner site in Glasgow did not know Guy Aldred's great resonant voice belabouring the evils of society. Hardly a Glasgow voter for three generations did not have the opportunity of electing him to the city or national government he despised so much, and vowed to enter only on his own terms if elected. But he never was elected, although he once stood simultaneously for fourteen city wards. He claimed there was better company in Barlinnie Prison (which he knew well) than in the Corridors of Power.

Guy Alfred Aldred was born on November 5th 1886, and died on 16th October 1963. He had just 10 pence in his pocket when he died. Boy-preacher, Social Democrat, Prisoner of Conscience, Conscientious Objector, Anarcho-Communist, orater, writer, publisher -- Guy Aldred never ceased struggling for those things in which he believed. He was part of Glasgow's history, and must never be forgotten.

ISBN 0 946487 19 7. Paperback. Price £6:95p.

ON THE TRAIL OF ROBERT SERVICE. G.W.

Lockhart. It is doubtful if any poet, except perhaps Robert Burns, has commanded such world-wide affection as Robert Service. It is doubtful if any verse has been more often recited than *The Shooting of Dan McGrew* and *The Cremation of Sam McGee*. Boy Scouts, learned Professors, armchair wanderers and active followers of the open road have all fallen under the spell of the man who chronicled the story of the Klondike Gold Rush. Too few know the story of the Scottish bank-clerk who became the Bard of the Yukon -- his early revolt against convention, his wandering vagabond years in the States and Canada, and his later travels in Tahiti and Russia.

This book tells the story of a man who captivated the imagination of generations, expressed the feelings and emotions of millions, and painlessly introduced countless numbers to the beauties of verse. Written with the full support of his family and containing some hitherto unpublished photographs, this book will delight Service lovers in both the Old World and the New.

ISBN   0 946487 24 3 Price: £5:95

SEVEN STEPS IN THE DARK. Bob Smith. The life and

times of a Scottish miner. Before it is too late, before the last Scottish miner has hung up his lamp for the last time, Bob Smith has recorded his lifetime's work in the mines of Scotland. He started work in the pit when he was fourteen, working with his father, when every ton of coal was cut by hand with a pick, when ponies dragged it to the shaft, and every penny of pay was fought for against a grasping coal-owner.

He saw his industry nationalised, then mechanised, and finally destroyed. He worked in the pits for forty years, until injury forced his retirement. He was an active Tades Unionist all his life, and a Lodge Official for many years. He experienced strikes, and was always at the sharp end of the struggle for safety and better conditionss. This is a miner's view of history, and records the reality behind the statistics and the rhetoric of politicians and managers and Trades Union officials.

ISBN   0 946487 21 9   Price: £8:95p.

REVOLTING SCOTLAND. Jeff Fallow

A book of cartoons, showing Scotland of yesterday and today.
GREETINGS FRAE BONNY SCOTLAND!
Yes, but which Scotland?
Definitely not the Scotland of Heilan' Flings, Porridge and Haggis.
Certainly not the Scotland of Kilty Dolls, Mean Jocks and Tartan Trivia.
This is Scotland as it is, and Scotland as it was, and Scotland as it will
be.
It is a book of cartoons, some very funny, some very bitter, and all very
true.
You might learn more about Scottish history from these cartoons than
you ever did at school.
If you are a visitor, you will understand more. If you are a Scot, you
might just feel like getting up and doing something about it.

ISBN 0946487 23 1. Paperback. 130 pages. Price £5:95p.

**Any of these books can be obtained from
your bookseller, or, in case of difficulty,
please send price shown, plus £1 for post
and packing, to:**

LUATH PRESS LTD.

BARR, AYRSHIRE. KA26 9TN

Tel: Barr (046-486) 636